Barry Christm

Lancashire Mining
Disasters

1835–1910

Wigan Colliery Lasses

'Bringing out the dead ...'

Lancashire Mining Disasters

1835–1910

JACK NADIN

MINING HERITAGE
SERIES

Series Editor
Brian Elliott

Wharncliffe Books

First Published in Great Britain in 2006 by
Wharncliffe Books
an imprint of
Pen and Sword Books Ltd
47 Church Street
Barnsley
South Yorkshire
S70 2AS

Copyright © Jack Nadin 2006

ISBN: 1 903425 95 6

Typeset in 10/12pt Palatino by Concept, Huddersfield.

Printed and bound in England by CPI UK

Pen and Sword Books Ltd incorporates the Imprints of
Pen & Sword Aviation, Pen & Sword Maritime,
Pen & Sword Military, Wharncliffe Books,
Pen & Sword Select, Pen and Sword Military Classics
and Leo Cooper.

For a complete list of Pen & Sword titles please contact
PEN & SWORD BOOKS LIMITED
47 Church Street
Barnsley
South Yorkshire
S70 2BR
England
E-mail: enquiries@pen-and-sword.co.uk
Website: www.pen-and-sword.co.uk

Contents

The Lancashire Coalfield and the area covered by this book. Author's collection

Foreword

There have been numerous studies concerning particular mining disasters but few regional and general accounts. *Lancashire Mining Disasters* is the first of what is hoped will be an authoritative series of publications.

Jack Nadin is a former miner with a great interest in mining history. Anyone reading his descriptions of the terrible events and circumstances surrounding the disasters will appreciate his empathy towards Lancashire miners.

Jack has included in his study details of thirty-six disasters, from the inrush of water at Ladyshore Colliery in 1835 to the explosion at No. 3 Bank Pit (Pretoria) on that dreadful December day in 1910. He also provides useful background information about each pit before and after each catastrophic event. Jack's research findings, including lists of fatalities, will be of interest to the increasing number of family historians with Lancashire mining ancestry.

Major mine disasters were always national news. From mid-Victorian times the big explosions attracted the interest of the *Illustrated London News* (founded in 1842), the first mass circulation journal dedicated to topical events. The horror associated with men and boys burnt, maimed and gassed, together with dreadful scenes of mass mourning were ideal subjects for graphic representation. Accounts of extraordinary bravery and rescue also captured the public imagination. By 1853 the *Illustrated London News* had published twenty mine disaster engravings. The original drawings, executed from eyewitness accounts and on the spot interpretation, were completed by artists of Royal Academy status. Competition to the *Illustrated London News* was provided by *The Graphic* who had the foresight to employ socially aware young artists. National, regional and local newspapers published detailed accounts of disasters, along with reports of inquests and lists of fatalities, information otherwise confined to official sources.

Despite all the media attention far more injuries and deaths occurred in day-to-day accidents, especially at the coal face. By the time of Senghenydd in 1913 average annual death rates had fallen to 1.3 per 1,000 (from over 4 per 1,000 in the 1850s) but of course statistics were no consolation to bereaved families. However, what made the big disasters such singular and catastrophic events was that a significant proportion of the male population of a mining settlement or village could be wiped out overnight, leaving scores of widows and hundreds of orphans. Some families were particularly hard hit, having lost loved ones in previous accidents or with several members killed in a single disaster. Public subscriptions and relief funds may have helped but there was no real compensation available for households already not far off poverty level. Perhaps the only parallel was the great local loss incurred by the close-knit Pals regiments on the Somme.

Jack Nadin's book is a welcome addition to our developing knowledge and appreciation of our social and industrial history and serves as a great tribute to Lancashire miners, their families and communities.

Brian Elliott

Introduction

Coal mining in Lancashire was a major employer from the early 1840s, when larger pits were being sunk to meet the ever-increasing demand of the Industrial Revolution. The hungry mills, factories, and foundries were crying out for coal which was to make England the greatest manufacturing nation in the world. It was coal that fuelled these industries and created the 'Great' in Great Britain. The factories, the foundries and steelworks supplied the world, but coal supplied the means of making these goods for export and home use. It was also from the early 1840s, that the terrible colliery disasters occurred, and continued to do so well into the twentieth century. In the early days, labour was cheap and so was life, and many men and boys perished in mining accidents. Most of these were caused by underground explosions when proper mining science was in its infancy, and lessons were slow to be learnt. Disaster after disaster wiped out hundreds, even thousands of lives, before the authorities and mine owners began to act. It is also true that many of the accidents were caused by the men and boys employed as

A typical mid-nineteenth century disaster scene, re-created by an artist from the Illustrated London News. www.cmhrc.co.uk

Mass funerals were an all too common occurrence following Victorian mining disasters.
www.cmhrc.co.uk

miners themselves. The Davy lamp, and others such makes, had safety features to prevent explosions and were readily available. But the miners hated the new safety lamp, which barely gave off enough light to see with, referring to it as a *'candle in a stocking'*. In the hands of the men, and in spite of locks and other devices to prevent opening, the tops of lamps were often taken off, even in gassy workings, or the gauze pricked to make a hole, exposing the flame, with terrible consequences. Sheets, known as brattice were erected underground to control and direct air currents but they were often taken down (once the underlooker was out of sight), being a hindrance to the working miner; consequently gasses accumulated and were ignited by the open lamps. Indeed, a number of mines continued to use naked flames, or candles, even in the gassiest of seams, both men and managers knowing full well the effects and danger involved in doing so.

Colliery explosions almost became a regular event, an accepted part of mining communities, where if you were not blasted into eternity, you would almost certainly be killed through roof falls, a haulage accident or in an over-winding incident at the pit shaft. In some cases special trains were organised to bring 'visitors and spectators' to view the events as they happened. In the main, it was the great underground explosions that took away most lives, and the victims included many of tender age, whose lives were extinguished before adult life had begun. Young lads of nine, ten and eleven years of age, employed in the pits as 'drawers', the term for taking the loaded coals to the pit shaft, were often the victims of major disasters. They were often the last out of the pit, having to take the labours of the collier to the pit bottom.

Officially, a 'disaster' is an accident that causes the death of ten or more persons, but I have included some accidents where less than ten have died, due to unusual circumstances, where a number of young innocent lives were lost, or where acts of great bravery took place. In fact, one of the first 'disasters', that of the Burgh Hall Colliery, falls into this category, for it shows the all too common breaches of the Coal Mines Acts which were passed by Parliament to protect the young and innocent from working underground in coal mines. Thankfully, colliery explosions did become less frequent as mining science improved, but in between gaining this knowledge, thousands died in the coalfields of Lancashire, as they did in other parts of the country. However, disasters did continue well into the 1960s with horrendous loss of lives.

In deep remembrance to those who died in these disasters – and in all mining accidents – these are the true stories of those who perished Lancashire's coal mines.

Acknowledgments

In writing about Lancashire's coal mining disasters, there are a number of persons and organisations to whom I am indebted for their help and assistance. These include the staff at several local reference libraries, including Wigan, Leigh, Westhoughton, St Helens, Burnley, Oldham, and Bolton. I thank them for their time and efforts in helping me, in particular for pointing out the locality of various pits, and giving me information that would otherwise have been difficult as a non local to their particular area to otherwise research; and for supplying all the information I asked for without question. Individuals who have also helped include Ian Winstanley of Ashton-in-Makerfield and his coal mining history website (www.cmhrc.co.uk); Alan Davies, Tyldesley; Harry Tootle, Oswaldtwistle; and Gordon Hartley, Burnley. My appreciation also goes to my wife, Rita, for all her time and patience for putting up with my absence while doing field studies, or when I was stuck in front of the computer typing away and for supplying much needed refreshments. Lastly, but not least, to Wharncliffe Books, without whom this publication would not have been possible. To anyone I have missed out, I also give a big thank you.

The Price of Coal.
Brian Elliott, from a sculpture
by Graham Ibberson

11

Old miner filling coal. Brian Elliott, from a scuplture by Graham Ibberson

Part One
The Early Colliery Disasters
1835–1852

(1) Ladyshore Colliery, Little Lever, Bolton: 10 July 1835

There was no hope whatsoever of the seven boys and ten men left underground ...

The Ladyshore Colliery was down Ladyshore Road at Little Lever, near Bolton and on the right-hand (west) side of the road, astride the Manchester, Bolton & Bury Canal. A reminder of the old colliery can be seen on Ladyshore Road, by way of the now extensively renovated Ladyshore House, which was formerly the pit manager's house. The nearby block of buildings (dated 1833) was used as part of the colliery offices, and as stabling for the pit ponies. Below the former colliery site the land dips steeply away to a large meander of the River Croal, and an area of flat land. Coal had been worked here for centuries. It has been speculated that the local cottagers were digging for the fuel in the late 1700s, and early 1800s. The Ladyshore Colliery is thought to have been in existence from around 1820, and by the 1890s was connected with the Farnworth Bridge Colliery about 1¼ miles away further down the Manchester, Bolton and Bury Canal. The colliery employed 315 persons in 1885, and was worked under John Fletcher Esqure, until 1930, when it went under the title of Ladyshore Coal Co. (1930) Ltd. of Ladyshore Colliery, Little Lever, Bolton.

There were forty men and boys at work in the Ladyshore Colliery at about eight o'clock on the morning of Friday 10 July 1835. William Hurst was attending to some wagons near the pit bottom, when he was startled by a great rush of wind through the workings of the mine. Immediately after, he heard the coal wagons being pushed down the tunnels that were a little further away from the shaft, and the rushing and roaring of torrents of water. He realised the pit was being inundated with water, and rushed headlong to the 'Ladder Pit' a short distance away. Others too were rushing the same way, seventeen of whom had been working in the lower seams, when they, too, became alarmed by the noise of rushing water. The surface workers on hearing the commotion from below, gazed down the embankment to the River Croal, and watched awe struck as a large cavity opened on its banks into which the full flow of the river plunged.

The pit, it was reported at the time, was 65 yards deep and, considering the steep slope below, running down to the River Croal, the workings must have been very shallow indeed. One person put the workings at *2 or 3 feet* below the surface. The cause of the inrush, however, was never really determined. Was it, as some thought caused through the water breaking into the old workings made by the cottagers long before, and then the water finding its way into those then worked by the pit? Or was it an error on behalf of the management? They refuted any blame, saying that as they approached the river, the workings then turned right, and no workings were ever under the river. However, the measuring devices used were primitive, working off levelling and the distance from the shaft. Mistakes could have been made, and if they were, it was at a massive human cost. The heavy rains in the previous days to the accident would not have helped matters, a deluge that continued for days afterwards and hindered the rescue operations. Little comments deserves to be made either of the great crowds that gathered around the pit following the accident – though, of course some of these would have been relatives and friends, but not all 10,000 of them! It was said that special trains were even laid on for the 'spectators' and each one was filled to capacity. There was no hope whatsoever of the seven men and ten boys still below ground; they had all drowned. What remained now was to get the bodies out, and do the decent thing.

Under the direction of John Fletcher, the owner of the colliery, fifty men were set to work beside the river and the hole into which the waters still flowed. A number of planks were placed over the opening in an attempt to stem the flow of water pouring into the pit, weighed down with hogsheads (large barrels) filled with stones to keep them in place. Two chain pumps were set to work by the steam-engine at the shaft, which worked relentlessly day and night. However, further heavy rains washed away the planking, and once again the river spewed into the workings of the mine. It was then decided to drive in piles of timber in a semi-circle, so as to provide a dam against the water. These were sealed with clay to make them watertight. They next began to pump out the water from behind the dam, and to make excavations down into the hole, and the pit itself. Here, on Wednesday 15 July, four days after the initial inrush, the recovery party came across the drowned body of a young man named James Greenhalgh. He was found on his face besides one of the pillars of coal. At half past eleven, the morning after, another man, named John Hurst, was found in the same part of the pit. By Saturday 25 July, two weeks after the flooding, the water in the shaft at the Ladyshore Colliery was still more than 30 yards deep. Some tools had been found belonging to a man named Rimmer, but no other bodies had been recovered. In the days that followed four others were found and, by 8 August, another nine bodies had been removed. This left just two bodies in the pit un-discovered, and by 15 August, all were out save that of the man named Rimmer. It was thought that he would have been one of the first to be discovered, as he was working near to where the water burst in. He was later found, and had been washed away by the force of the river to a remote part of the workings.

A full list of names of those who perished at the Ladyshore Colliery was not published, just those mentioned above were identified. Only an extensive search through parish records and burial records *might* reveal the rest. It is likely that we may never know for certain who died that day, or even how the accidents happened.

By 1938, the Ladyshore 'Owlhole', 'Victoria' and the Farnworth Collieries were employing 208 men underground and 114 surface workers. Time was running out however, and just over a decade later the pit was abandoned, in July 1949, according to the National Coal Board records. At the time of the closure the colliery employed 236 men, and the last full year's output was 39,541 tons. The closure must have been a somewhat hurried affair, since canal boats were left at the canal-side as if waiting to be loaded and, in a shed near the colliery, a barge was turned on its side waiting to be re-planked. A reclamation scheme was begun in 1981 around the site of the former pit, and in the valley below where the water burst into the pit, with its horrific consequences. The original cobbled roadway, Ladyshore Road, was retained on the site. This once led down to Lever Bank Bleach works and the Nova Brickworks. It was coal mining also that caused the breach in the canal a little further on past the former colliery, in 1936. The casual walker here along the tow-path is obliged to walk along the canal bed, where the breach is clearly visible, although somewhat overgrown now. When the breach did occur, it took with it two of the canal barges. A number of sunken barges could be seen along this stretch of the canal up to around the late 1970s. Ladyshore is now a peaceful site, trees and shrubs were planted, and bullfinches and chaffinches dart and dive along the canal that took Ladyshore coal in times past. Dragonflies flit and hover, and all is tranquil now – as if time has forgotten the terrible events of 170 years ago. All that remains today is a silent reminder of the old shaft, a sunken hollow on the far side of the canal. An information board nearby gives some information about the disaster.

(2) Burgh Colliery: 24 November 1846

... each must have known that death was near for when found they were clasped in each other's arms ...

The years 1841 and 1842, saw the publication of the *Reports of the Royal Commission on the Employment of Children in Mines*, which gave a startling insight to the terrible conditions underground endured by the miners and, in particular, their young families. The Bill became law in August 1842 and, following this, no females were allowed to work underground in a coal mine, and no young boys under the age of ten years. At this time it was common practice and even accepted that the miner hewed the coal, and his family helped in getting the coal to the shaft bottom – effectively supplementing the family income. The Bolton colliers, not far away from Coppull, complained:

> That those who know nothing of the working classes, were taking the bread out of their mouths.

Unfortunately, there was little or no provision to put the new law into effect, and as a consequence females and male children under the age of ten years old continued to be employed in the mines for many years to come and this happened at the Burgh Colliery, Coppull.

The Burgh Colliery was in beautiful countryside near the village of Coppull to the south of Chorley. The pit was sunk about 1836, and at the time of this disaster was worked by John Hargreaves, a respected gentleman, Justice of the Peace and Magistrate, who lived in Bolton. The shaft here was said to have been over the River Yarrow, which today would have been down Sunny Brow in the village, just over the bridge on the river, now part of the Yarrow Nature Trail. The numerous pits in this area were eventually all connected underground and went under the collective title of Coppull Collieries. These included shafts or pits named Dry Bones, Dry Dam, Burgh, as well as Coppull Colliery itself. The shaft at the Burgh Pit was sunk to a depth of 154 yards. At the bottom of the shaft was a main tunnel sloping away to the south-east about 70 yards in length. Although the Burgh Colliery was owned by John Hargreaves, he took little interest in the running of the mine, leaving this task to Thomas Grime, who acted as the assistant mining engineer and fireman at the pit. Grime was assisted in his duties by Thomas Halliwell until a few months before the explosion, when Halliwell insisted that he

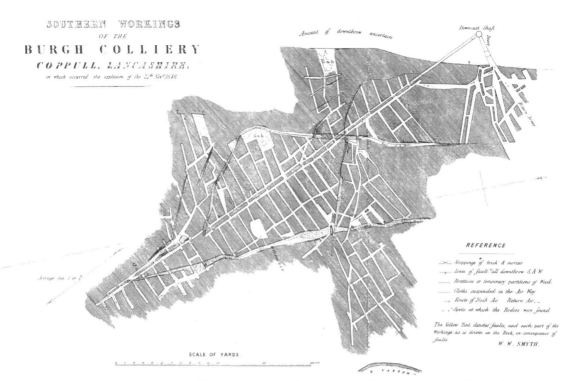

The workings at the Burgh Colliery at the time of the accident. From the reports of the mines inspectors. Author's collection

went back to his former job, that of a collier (on more pay), which he did, leaving Thomas solely responsibility of running the pit.

Contrary to the rules of the pit, and those of the Act of 1842, which was well known to all employed in coal mines, Thomas Halliwell introduced his daughter, along with another young girl, into the pit to act as drawers or waggoners, for him, dressing them up in male attire. The fact that he did this makes it known that he was well aware of the rules. This was soon noticed of course, but most 'turned a blind eye' and went about their own business, of working the coal and earning money to keep the family in bread. It was a Mr Jackson, the surveyor for the owner of the mine, who informed John Hargreaves about the violation of rules. Hargreaves set off for Coppull immediately, and summoned Halliwell before him. Thomas Halliwell flatly denied the offence, or any knowledge of it. Hargreaves was not convinced, but could prove little. Hargreaves laid down the law, and told Halliwell that if he, or anyone else employed by him, should be proved to have committed the offence, then they would be instantly dismissed. However, Halliwell continued his violation.

Part of Thomas Grime's duty, as fireman at the pit, was to descend the mine before the men, and inspect the workings for gas or falls of roof. When each working place was found to be safe, Grime would place a lighted candle there, an indication to the man due to be working that all was safe, the area having been inspected. Thomas Grime would descend the pit around a half hour before the men to make his inspection, and the men would have followed in half an hour later. This was the order of events on Tuesday 24 November 1846, but on this day, Fireman Grime was a little behind his normal schedule. The first of the workmen to enter the part of the mine not yet inspected was the former fireman, Thomas Halliwell who, knowing the rules, should have stayed clear until his workings had been inspected by Grime and a candle lit at that place. He chose not to do so, lit his own candle and an explosion took place. As soon as the blast was known on the surface, the agent for Mr Hargreaves, a man named Mr Ellis, immediately descended the shaft, and courageously went with lamp in hand to the place where the explosion had occurred. Before he could reach the spot, the foul air and lack of oxygen extinguished his lamp, but on hearing groans, he obtained another light.

He went forward again, and found the fireman (Mr Grime) alive who, with the assistance of others, was then conveyed to the shaft and raised to the pit bank. Here Grime was attended to by Mr Smith, the surgeon from Chorley, and then taken to his residence. In the meantime, another explosion occurred, not as violent as the first, but enough to slow down the recovery operations. Rescue work soon resumed, and the next person to be found was the body of Thomas Halliwell, the person who had caused the blast. He was found about 35 yards away from where Grime was found, and about 200 yards from the pit bottom. He was beyond help, yet not very much burnt, save for his back. He was without his shirt, as if ready to start work, and appeared like the rest to have been making his way out of the pit, when overcome by the afterdamp, the deadly gas left by an explosion. Next, the body of Seth Turner, aged twenty-three, was found. He, too, had suffocated in the afterdamp. William Wilding was found next, aged about sixteen, a drawer who, having his shirt off ready for work, was much burnt about the body since he was caught in the initial blast, and then overcome by the afterdamp.

The forth body was that of Jane Halliwell, Thomas's daughter, aged just thirteen years. Although not much burnt, she had died through suffocation by the after-damp. The next two bodies were those of Joseph Hale, aged fourteen years, and little Mary Booth, the other girl Halliwell had brought underground to work for him, aged only eleven years. Both these youngsters appeared not to be burnt at all, but each must have known death was near for when found they were clasped in each other's arms, as if to be comforting each other, before the deadly gas snuffed away their tiny young lives. The seventh body to be recovered was that of William Turner, aged twenty-three, burnt around the neck and arms, and suffocated. The eighth and last of the victims was Jane Moss, another female and a drawer at the pit who was also suffocated.

The inquest into the deaths at the Burgh Colliery took place at the *Wheatsheaf* public house at Coppull before Richard Palmer, the Preston coroner. After some deliberation and adjournment, the jury give the verdict of *Accidental death* in all cases. Thomas Grime did not survive more than a few days after the explosion, bringing the total number killed in this sad accident to nine. The owner of the Burgh Colliery, John Hargreaves, was later taken to court for allowing the children to work below ground. Hargreaves, himself a magistrate, claimed that he took no part in the day-to-day running of the mine, and employed persons of more experience to perform this work. Thomas Grime, the fireman, was dead, so the court fined Hargreaves's agent, Mr Ellis, a pitiful ten shillings, just over a shilling a life, after which the case was dismissed.

Victims of the Burgh Colliery Disaster were:

Thomas Grime, fireman
Thomas Halliwell, collier, aged 37
Seth Turner, collier, aged 23
William Wilding, drawer, aged 'about sixteen'.
Jane Halliwell, drawer, daughter to Thomas Halliwell, aged 13
Joseph Hale, drawer, aged 14
Mary Booth, drawer, aged 11 years
William Turner, collier, aged 25
Jane Moss, a drawer, age not specified

The Coppull Colliery, which included the Burgh Pit, appears to have been abandoned around 1862. This was just ten years after another fatal explosion at was what named the 'Coppull New Pit', with even more disastrous consequences (page 32), taking away thirty-six lives. In 1844 a locomotive, named *Sans Pareil* was taken to the Coppull Colliery, and adapted for use as a stationary engine, used to drive the pumping and winding machinery at the pit, where it worked until 1862, when Coppull was finally abandoned. *Sans Pareil* was later re-erected as a locomotive and presented to the Science Museum.

(3) Haydock Colliery, 6 March 1850

... they came across more and more dead men and boys, each more or less dreadfully burned ...

The Haydock Colliery was located at Haydock, near St Helens, and was worked by Messrs Evans and Turner, the forerunner of Richard Evans and Sons, the major colliery proprietor around Haydock and Ashton-in-Makerfield. The Haydock Colliery was part of the Lancashire Section in the *Report on Child Labour in Coal Mines* taken in 1841, which gave a vivid insight of the working conditions of the miners, and the women and children employed underground at this time. Here is a typical extract:

[DINAH BRADBURY, waggoner at Mr. Evan's Haydock Colliery, May 19, 1841]
What age are you? – *I cannot tell you, to tell the truth, but I think I am between 18 and 19 years old.*
You are a drawer I believe? – *Yes, I am; I draw for two men, but one of them was hurt himself, so I am out soon today.*
Do you use the belt and chain? – *No, we don't need them, we have rails laid in these pits; the rails are laid up to every man's place, and we waggon between them.*
What length of hours do you work? – *I go down between four and five o'clock in the morning, and I come up between five and six in the evening.*
Do you ever work at night? – *No, we never work in these pits at night.*
Have you any small children in the pits? – *Oh, yes, a deal.*
Have you any time for meals? – *We generally stop to eat when we have time, and generally find time.*
At what age do you intend to turn us out of the pit? – *Put me down 15 years old – I should like to be turned out.*

Do you not like your present employment? – *No, I don't, and I would not go down if I could get anything else to do.*

According to the first reports on this disaster, the pit was 'Situated in Haydock about a mile and a half from the lunatic asylum, and nearly the same distance from Newton race ground.' Rock Pit was about 240 yards deep, and was one of a number at the Haydock Colliery. The underlooker at the Colliery, Thomas Litherland, deposed that he was down the No. 13 Pit at the time of the disaster, indicating the number of pits there. It was common for the men at the Haydock Collieries to use naked flames (candles) even though there had been a number of explosions at the Haydock pits in recent years. Although the flame safety lamp was at this time becoming more widespread, with all its benefits, it was almost universally disliked by the miners – they called it 'A candle in a stocking.'

The men at the Rock Pit descended at around four o'clock in the morning, as was usual, and following the inspection of the workings by the fireman, proceeded to their place of work. Eleven men were at their stalls getting the coal about 1,000 yards from the pit bottom, another two were about 950 yards nearer the shaft, making a total of thirteen men in the inner workings of the pit. Five others were working near the shaft, shunting the coals and raising it to the surface. Just a dozen yards below them were a number of other men mining from a different seam. The men had been at work barely two hours, when around six o'clock there was an explosion. Moses Litherland, the son of the underlooker, Thomas Litherland, had just been to the far end of the workings with his pony, and was returning to a spot about 400 yards from the shaft when the explosion occurred.

At the No. 13 Pit, the underlooker, Thomas Litherland, was aware something had happened, as the air was becoming foul with the afterdamp, so he signalled and was raised up the pit. He made his way over to the Rock Pit and descended, finding two men, Richard Houghton and John Clarke, who had gone down before him, and had already found a number of men and boys dead. Progress into the further workings was stopped by the afterdamp, but the air was resuming its proper course, and in about half an hour they were able to proceed. As they began to move forward, they came across more and more dead men and boys, each more or less dreadfully burned, scorched upon body and limbs, along with a number of dead ponies.

Two of the men who were working nearer the shaft heard the explosion, and appeared in their confusion to have run towards the blast – whether to help others, or in simple confusion, we will now never know. They were discovered overcome and suffocated by the deadly afterdamp. After a prolonged and extensive search, the final death toll at the Rock Pit that fateful Saturday morning was put at thirteen men and boys. One man, John Sims, had his head blown almost completely off by the force of the explosion. The youngest lad was just eleven years of age. Those who died that day, were named as:

Ralph Unsworth, collier, aged 46 years, who left a wife and four children
John Unsworth, drawer, aged 19 years, singleman
John Dearden, collier, aged 44 years, who left a wife and six children
Ralph Dearden, drawer, aged 17, singleman

Bringing the dead out of the shafts at Haydock Colliery. From The Graphic, *29 June 1878.*
www.cmhrc.co.uk

William Battesby, collier, aged 47 years, who left a wife and four children
Christopher Hesketh, drawer, aged 18 years, singleman
John Sims, collier, aged 20 (who was dreadfully injured)
John Gleave, collier, aged 39 years, who left a wife and five children
John Holloway, drawer, aged 18
Joseph Houghton, a pony driver, aged 14 years
Thomas Glover, drawer, aged 11 years
James Bailey, drawer, aged 15 years (who was dreadfully mangled)
William Knowles, waggoner, aged 25 years, who left a wife and one child.

The inquest on the disaster at the Rock Pit of the Haydock Collieries was held a few days later and, after examining several witnesses, returned the following verdict:

It so happened that the foul and inflammable air in the said coal mine, by some means unknown to the jury, took fire accidentally, casually, and by some misfortune exploded, whereby the above named unfortunate men and boys were grievously scorched and burned upon the body and limbs, whereby they instantly died.

There was no recommendation to men or management by the jury that in future only flame safety lamps should be used at the Rock Pit.

(4) Bent Grange Colliery, 9 October 1850

Upon tables, trestles, barrels and planks disfigured and burnt bodies of the unfortunate men and boys littered the room.

This pit was worked by Thomas Butterworth from around the mid 1840s, and the colliery was abandoned circa 1869. During its short life the Bent Grange Colliery was the scene of two major mining disasters, which claimed the lives of thirty-six men and boys. The colliery is shown to have had just one shaft on a map of 1851, although a report below stated that a new shaft was being sunk in 1850. The Royley Mine was worked at Bent Grange at a depth of 222 yards. A boiler house was located some distance away, and close to this was a reservoir that supplied the water to the engine.

'On the surface there was an absence of that order and regularity which is seen in connection with larger concerns' stated a report in July 1853.

The Bent Grange Colliery was in the location of the present Grange Art Centre, Oldham, where close by, there is also a 'Grange Street'. Ventilation at the Bent Grange Pit at this time was implemented by partitioning the shaft into two sections with timbers and brattice cloth. The winding-engine turned a fan of 3 feet diameter, which forced air into the workings, but only when winding was in operation. At other times water raised from the workings was turned back down the mineshaft to cause ventilation current. However, the men at Bent Grange all felt that the ventilation circuit was adequate. In 1849 the shaft was sunk further to a depth of 221 yards to make contact with the Riley Mine. The pit workings were then opened out in a North and South direction on either side of the shaft. By October 1850, the South Level was about 140 yards from the shaft and the North Level around 60 yards from the shaft. The workings were of the 'Pillar and Stall' method whereby 3 feet pillars were left to support the roof, the coal between (the Stall) was taken to a width of 8 or 9 feet, and around 5 feet high. A new shaft was in the process of being sunk as a downcast shaft and was around 40 yards deep.

A new fan for this shaft of 9 feet in diameter had been ordered. On Wednesday 9 October 1850 a tremendous thunderstorm beat down on the Manchester and Oldham Districts accompanied by sheets of lightening and heavy downpours of rain. Around a quarter past one that day, Thomas Newton, of Edge Lane, Royton, a collier at the pit, was walking away from the shaft having finished his work for the day, when he heard a 'rush of wind up the pit'. His instant reaction was that the pit had fired, and he and others with him ran back to the pit mouth. Over 600 feet below ground in the shaft lay mayhem and destruction. The cloth and timber partition had been blown down by the blast deep within the bowels of the earth, and yet there was no loud report as would be expected from a colliery explosion. Smoke, soot and a sulphurous yellow cloud now drifted up from the silent hell in the workings far below. Forty-two men and boys had entered the workings at Bent Grange Colliery that morning, and as a number had made their way out of the pit prior to the explosion, the management had little idea who was still down the pit. Thomas Butterworth, the colliery owner, was in the town and a mere 500 or 600 yards from the pit when he heard of the disaster, and was on the scene within minutes. His first priority was for those underground, for saving lives, or at least getting those less fortunate creatures to the surface. The foreman, William Lane, along with another person descended the smoke-filled shaft in a makeshift hopper.

Slowly, into the depths the hopper was lowered, until at 80 yards below the surface the signal was given to raise the men back to the surface. The foulness of the air in the shaft prevented any further exploration for around an hour, when another attempt was made. The basket was lowered to within 7 or 8 yards of the pit shaft bottom, when they were compelled to leave it and make their way through a mass of tangled timber and brattice cloth that blocked further progression. With difficulty they wormed their way through the blockage and, with means of a rope, completed their hazardous journey. Near the mouth of the shaft they found John Jones, John Lane, Daniel Dunkerley and several others, all burnt, bruised and in shock. The rescuers sent these men up the pit, before searching for others. At the top of a small tunnel some 5 or 6 yards from the shaft they came across the six dead bodies of their companions. The air in this part of the mine, although only yards from the shaft, was too thick and un-breathable to carry on. The two rescuers retreated and were drawn to the surface. The foreman, William Lane, was so exhausted on arrival at the surface that he collapsed and had to be removed to his home where he remained ill for some time. The scene on the surface of the colliery must have presented a pitiful sight as hundreds of mourners gathered in the downpour awaiting news of their loved ones. Seeing the effects of the foul air on the rescuers, the men on the surface were disinclined to follow the rescue attempts in the underground holocaust.

Mr Butterworth put forward offers of a bonus (yet refused to go himself!) to the gathering of miners. Samuel Scholes and a man named Nathan presented themselves, and within a short time succeeded in sending up William Greenhalgh, alive but a little injured with burns on his back and legs. The rescuers were again forced to retreat from the workings due to foul air. Around 4 pm William Mason and a man named Geary made yet another attempt to go into the pit workings and managed to succeed in getting Daniel Dunkerley, still alive, to the part of the shaft blocked by debris. Daniel was a bulky, tall man, and unable to get through the small aperture in the timbers through to the hopper. William Mason returned to the surface and returned down the pit with a ladder, but by the time they had got back down to Dunkerley he was dead. Leaving Daniel where he lay, the pair made renewed efforts to find anyone who was still alive. Gearly, found the body of his

Rescue workers descend the shaft at Bent Grange Colliery, searching for survivors. From a print that would be typical of the scene, Illustrated London News, *29 September 1878.* www.cmhrc.co.uk

24

brother, Edward, dead, some 7 or 8 yards from the bottom of the pit shaft. Other would-be rescuers had now plucked up courage, and more hasty attempts were made to find any of those still alive. Two or three men were found alive and sent out of the pit, but beyond a few yards from the shaft the air was totally unbreathable. Rescue was again halted. Between ten and eleven o'clock at night, William Mason again descended into the workings, and was able to find alive George Clough near the mouth of the shaft. He was brought up the pit. Intermittent explorations between then and five o'clock in the morning by William Mason, Thomas Mason, Benjamin Roberts and William Beswick recovered a further nine dead bodies, many within yards of the shaft bottom.

Rescuers descended into the sump hole where the mine water collects at the shaft bottom and found the dead bodies of three boys: Jonas Fox, Bartholomew Bambling and James Parkin. During the course of the following day several more dead men and boys were recovered, until at last, at five o'clock that evening on examination of a list of men employed, only one man was missing. Edmund Butterworth, married and about forty years of age was to be the last victim of the Bent Grange Colliery Disaster to remain underground. The dead men already recovered were removed through the grieving crowds to the *White Hart*, Low Moor, the injured conveyed home for treatment. More pitiful scenes surrounded the *White Hart* where fourteen bodies were laid out in an upper room as friends became anxious to see and identify those who had suffered. The room presented a spectacle not easily described. Upon tables, trestles, barrels, and planks disfigured and burnt bodies of the unfortunate men and boys littered the room. Some defied identification, while other had little if any marks upon their bodies, almost as if they were asleep. One poor little fellow (Bartholomew Bambling) aged just twelve years, had lost his left eye, as well as his life, probably as a consequence of being hurled against the side of the workings by the force of the blast.

A public subscription was set up for the relief of the widows and orphans, Joseph Saxon pledged an immediate twenty guineas to the fund.

When the explosion occurred several men and boys were at the bottom of the shaft, getting into the cage, and these escaped uninjured. One boy was said to have seized hold of the cage as it was going up but, after clinging for about 7 or 8 yards, fell and was killed.

The total death toll of the Bent Grange Colliery Disaster was put at sixteen, and were:

Bartholomew Bambling, drawer, aged 12
Thomas Bramwell, drawer, 21or 22
Edmund Butterworth, 40, who left a wife and five children
James Butterworth, 21, married (brother of owner of pit?)
Daniel Dunkerley, 31, left a wife and child
Robert Fidiham, 25, who left a wife and two children
Benjamin Fox, 34, who was married, no children
Jonas Fox, drawer, 17 (his brother)
Edward Geary, 32, wife and three children
James Jackson, 54 married, no children
William Lees, 32, wife and two children

Ralph Mytton, from Wigan, only in Oldham about one month.
George Newton, drawer,19
John Newton, drawer, aged 19
John Parkin, drawer, aged 13
John Stott, 47, wife and six children

A number of men and boys survived the disaster, although they suffered minor burns and other injuries. The Bent Grange Colliery claimed another twenty men and boys in an explosion on 1 July 1853. It is sad to say, that as far as I know, there is no memorial to those who perished in this, or the other Bent Grange Colliery Disaster, in the town.

(5) Ince Colliery, 22 December 1851

Half an hour later the pit exploded taking with it thirteen lives.

The Ince Colliery, the property of Messrs A H Haliburton at the time of this disaster was located near the Hindley station of the Lancashire and Yorkshire Railway, in a north-west direction from Highfield Road and its junction with Hall Lane. A tourist attraction in the shape of two 'burning wells' existed in Hindley, until the latter part of the nineteenth century, which was caused by the natural seepage of inflammable coal gas, or methane through water. The Ince Colliery had a tramway with the Penny Gate Colliery near Penny Gate Farm. There were a number of 'coal pits' and 'old coal pits' around here at the time of this disaster. Today, the site of the Ince Colliery has been taken by the Hindley Golf Club, although Penny Gate Farm still survives. The Ince Colliery was also known locally and variously as 'Deep Pit' as it was 1,242 feet deep, 'Arley Mine' from the seam it worked, and even 'Brown's Pit' from a former owner. The colliery was a major local employer, and at this time found work for upwards of 100 men and boys. Underground, the workings were divided into four distinct workings – but all in the same seam. Ventilation at the Ince Colliery was achieved by a furnace placed at the upcast shaft, and the normal procedure at weekends was to 'damp' the furnace down, or even let it go out, effectively leaving the pit all weekend with no ventilation at all. In any case, the furnace power appears to have been limited, the bars of the furnace being just 23 inches wide; however, the pit was deemed to be well ventilated by those who worked there.

The ventilation was so good, that most of the men worked by naked flames or candles. The Davy lamps were only used for inspections for gas by the firemen. The fact that the furnace was allowed to go out over the weekend, appears to have been a main factor in this explosion since this allowed gas to build up in the workings. On the Monday morning of 22 December 1851, just a few days before Christmas, at half past five, upwards of one hundred men and boys descended into the workings of the Ince Colliery to begin their day's work. Half an hour later the pit exploded taking with it thirteen lives. The explosion was confined to a portion of the pit furthest away from the furnace ventilation system, where a long straight tunnel had been driven with old and abandoned workings at each side. Most of these old workings had been barred off with gates and brattice cloth, effectively sealing them, and any gasses accumulating therein. One of them

Crowds gather at the pit top, Ince Colliery, women weeping for their loved ones. A typical scene, taken from the Illustrated London News, *31 June 1880.* www.cmhrc.co.uk

however, was not sealed off, and it was presumed that the lack of ventilation had allowed the gasses to escape and come into contact with one of the men's candles, with the inevitable results. Those who died (and their dependants) that day at the Ince Colliery were:

Robert Davies, aged 25, who left a widow and four small children, the eldest not even eleven years of age. He had been blown a considerable distance from the place where he worked.

Henry Meadows, aged 25, who left a widow who was expecting, and another child

Joseph Topping, 39, who left a widow and four children

John Topping, 15, son of Joseph

Henry Topping, 11, brother to John, and son of Joseph

John Hiram, or Aran, 45, leaving a widow bearing a child, and six other children

Elisha Hiram, or Aran, 15, a drawer, son of the above

John Whittle, 47, who left a widow and six children

Wright Southern, 15, a drawer

Matthew Edge, 15, a drawer

James Jolley, 15, a drawer

George Pigot, 65, a pit-bottom man. He was dreadfully burnt, and his head smashed. He left a widow.

Thomas Bushell, aged 21, unmarried.

Joseph Dickinson, the Mines Inspector, was at the inquest that followed. Joseph was most thorough whenever attending accidents and disasters, possibly more than any other inspector; he was totally committed to trying to end what almost amounted to carnage in the pits. At the first hearing, he asked for an adjournment on account that he had not been able to examine the pit following the disaster. After inspection he was able, with utmost accuracy, to pin-point the area in which the explosion had taken place. With remarkable experience in these matters, he put forward his theories as to how the disaster had occurred. He noted that pit props in the area of the seat of the explosion were thickly coated with dust, some even charred, and that the direction of the blast could be clearly traced and defined:

> The accumulation of gas in that wide tunnel was not only possible, but also probable. Pigot, the fireman for the district in which the explosion occurred, and who had died in the blast, was an old man. Although he is said to have been strong for his age, it appears questionable to me, how far a man so much advanced in age should be entrusted with duties which required more experience and care. It may have been that the fireman considered he had finished his examination, and had taken the top off his lamp, for the sake of more light.

The coroner, in addressing the jury, expressed his regret that they had no more definite evidence to guide them. Under the circumstances, he thought that no person alive could be charged with having caused the accident, and the jury, it appeared to him, must record a verdict of *Accidental Death*. After a few minutes consulting, the verdict was returned in compliance with the coroner's directions.

(6) Norley Hall Colliery: 22 April 1852

... the men on the pit bank were alarmed by a violent rush of air ...

The extraordinary rapidity at which colliery disasters were happening in Lancashire, and the country as a whole at this time, and the subsequent and terrible loss of life might, you may think, have caused the colliers to exercise more caution. Following an explosion at the Norley Hall Colliery on the 9 January 1852, by which six persons perished, and which was less than a month after the afore-mentioned Ince Colliery disaster, the Davy lamp was supplied to all the men and boys employed at the Norley Pit. Strict orders were also given that no naked candles were to be used, and that no one was allowed to take the top off their lamps. However, these rules appeared to have been totally ignored and, once more, through the reckless actions of the colliers themselves, they paid the highest of tolls: death.

The Norley Hall Colliery, worked by the executors of the late John Daglish, was located near Pemberton, Wigan. Norley Hall, the building, was at Kit Green to the north of the Ormskirk Road above Lamberhead Green near Pemberton. There were a number of 'coal pits' to the east of Kit Green and Norley Hall in the mid 1840s, which may have developed to become the Norley Hall Colliery.

The site of Norley Hall today is mainly open space around Pemberton School and its playing fields. The colliery consisted of two shafts: the engine pit, where the men and coal was raised, and an upcast or bye pit, where the ventilation furnace was placed. The engine pit was 160 yards deep, and from the bottom an inclined roadway was driven NNE for a distance of 250 yards to some air doors that controlled the ventilation circuit. Here, the inner workings of the pit branched off in a north and south direction. It was in the northern workings that the explosion of January 1852 took place with the loss of six lives. In the southern direction, the workings had been driven to the boundary of the estate of Reece Bevan, a distance of about 750 yards from the bottom of the engine pit. From here, the coal was being extracted back towards the shaft, and the roof behind was allowed to drop, resulting in what in mining terms is named the 'gob' or 'waste'. The coal seam being worked was that known as the Wigan Four Foot. The normal procedure at the colliery was that the men, who numbered between fifty and sixty employed at the pit, would wait at the point near the air doors, while the underlookers inspected the workings.

When this was done, and all declared safe, the men would be assigned to their various tasks for the day. The fireman was then supposed to check each lamp as the miners passed through the air doors. Once the colliers had finished their work for the day, they were allowed to leave the pit, but the drawers stayed on to remove the coal to the shaft bottom. By three o'clock on Friday afternoon, 22 April 1852, there were about twenty to twenty-five men remaining in the pit. At half past three, the men on the pit bank were alarmed by a violent rush of air, laden with slack and dirt, which shot up the engine pit shaft. Although there was no loud report, it was obvious that the pit had fired. The overlooker, William Twiss, and the underlooker, a man named Cuerden, were in a cabin at the time on the surface and they ran towards the pit mouth. After gathering what information they could, and that no damage had been done to the shaft or the cages, they began to organise the rescue operation. Cuerden, and a man named Taylor were the first to descend, about twenty-five minutes after the explosion.

William Twiss soon followed with a number of volunteers, and men from the adjoining collieries – as in all colliery disasters, there was no lack of willing hands. The point down to the air doors was found to be unaffected by the explosion, the ventilation was sluggish, but no afterdamp was evident. Through the air doors where they had expected to find a man named Leadbeater, the searchers split up, and a 'stopping' was repaired with some cloth to restore the ventilation. About 150 yards further on, they saw the body of the first victim, a boy named Thomas Farrimond, but the afterdamp here was so thick and he could not be reached. William Twiss ordered the rescue workers back to the air doors, and arranged the searchers into groups, making sure that each group had at least one man who worked at the pit and was familiar with the workings.

A fresh set of men was sent to recover the body of Thomas Farrimond. He was a door tenter and, such was the confusion, it was thought he was already out of the pit. As the rescue parties could not continue in the direction they had hoped due to the afterdamp, they altered their course passing through some side workings, restoring 'stoppings' as they moved forward, and the normal ventilation slowly resumed. Soon they found about twenty persons, nearly all boys, who were all got out alive, save three who were beyond hope. The man named Leadbeater who the searchers had hoped to find through the air doors, was recovered between eight

Many funerals took place following the disaster at Norley Hall. A typical scene taken from the Illustrated London News, *3 February 1849.* www.cmhrc.co.uk

and nine o'clock at night but he was dead. By midnight the search was over, and the following list was posted of the dead and injured at the pit gates where large crowds had gathered to await the news:

Dead
Peter Leadbeater, drawer, aged 33, dead when brought out
Thomas Hitchen, aged 15, dead when brought out, frightfully injured about the head
   and neck, head almost severed from the body
Edward Greenall, aged 14
Thomas Ashurst, aged 13, dead when brought out
Robert Roby, aged 12
Joseph Hitchen, aged 11, brother to Thomas, named above
John Lowe, aged 12

James Greenall, aged 15, brother to Edward named above
William Atherton, aged 13
William Huyton, aged 13

Injured
James Hitchen, collier, aged 40, father of the two boys on the above list, in a dying state
John Topping, aged 10, in a dangerous state
Adam Winyard, aged 10, badly burnt
William Darbyshire, aged 16, in a dangerous state
Thomas Farrimond, aged 10, badly burnt
James Atherton, aged 25, collier, much burnt
James Leadbeater, aged 28, collier, dangerous bruised or 'blown' rather than burnt.

Joseph Hitchen, the father of the two lads who died in the disaster, did in fact die from his wounds, as did William Darbyshire. This brought the total of those killed at the Norley Hall Colliery to twelve. The reason for the number of young lads who perished in the explosion is that they had to remain behind to draw the coals to the shaft, once the colliers had left. The inquest into the disaster was held at the *Red Lion* at Pemberton, and heard some conflicting evidence. Witnesses spoke of lamps that were locked, and the tops securely fixed. Others spoke of lamps that were rarely or never locked. Some said that candles were never used, others said that candles were used, or lamps with their tops off. The inquest was adjourned a couple of times, until the final verdict was announced:

The jury has come to the conclusion that according to the evidence adduced at this inquest, the verdict cannot be any other than 'Accidental death'. At the same time, we are strongly of the opinion, that there has been a gross mismanagement in carrying on the workings of the colliery, and great inconsistency in the evidence given as to the use of naked candles in the mine. And the jury consider it imperatively necessary on the part of the proprietors, that the rules and regulations should be strictly attended to, and that the instructions of Mr Wynne [Mines Inspector] should be carried out.

It is not known when the Norley Hall Colliery was abandoned, but in June 1865, there was a report that

Upwards of fifty men were imprisoned at the No. 2 Pit belonging to the Norley Hall Coal Co., at Pemberton near Wigan through a fall of brickwork in the shaft.

And on Wednesday 15 October 1890, it was reported that

A lamentable accident occurred in the No. 2 Pit Norley Colliery, on Monday afternoon, to Ralph Peters, a collier's drawer, engaged in the 6ft. mine. Peters was caught by a fall of roof – under which his father had just passed – but was immediately got out and conveyed to the surface. Two of the officials rendered first aid, and he was conveyed to his home in Victoria-street, Lamberhead Green, on the ambulance. The usefulness of the instruction gained in the Ambulance Classes was demonstrated in this case, for had not such aid been given the injured man could hardly have been got home alive. Dr. Griffiths, assistant to Dr. Molyneux, was early in attendance, and afterwards Dr. Graham and Dr. Griffiths treated the case, but it was considered advisable that he should be removed to the Infirmary, and the horse ambulance was obtained for the purpose. Peters had sustained a very severe injury to the thigh bone, the bone being cut through, and mischief done to the femoral artery. As stated, the injured man was conveyed to the Infirmary, but he died at eleven o'clock on Monday night.

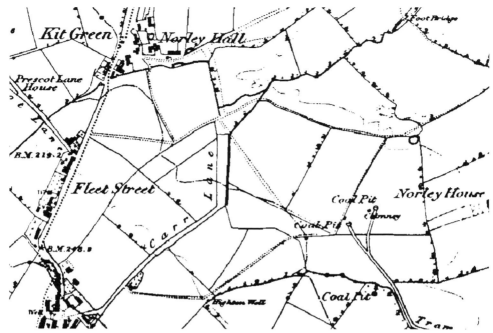

'Coal pits' around Norley House and Norley Hall are evident on this extract from an OS map surveyed 1844–48. Courtesy of the Ordnance Survey

This may have spelled the end of the pit, for it is not listed in a list of coal mines for the year 1890, or in any subsequent lists. The Catalogue of Plans of Abandoned Mines does mention the pit, but gives little other information.

(7) Coppull Hall Colliery: 20 May 1852

Those on the surface of the mine saw a fearful rush of dust-laden air shoot up the shaft skywards.

We have already related to the events at the Burgh Pit of the Coppull Colliery, whereby eight persons died, including two females who were illegally employed. There were no lessons learnt from that disaster, since in this explosion of 1852 a further thirty-six lives were lost, including two lads below the legal age for working underground, one aged nine years, and the other the pitiful age of seven. The Coppull Hall Colliery was still in the hands of John Hargreaves, who now lived at Southport, whilst the running of the pit was still in the hands of a pit manager, a man named Ellis. There were four or five pits working collectively as 'Coppull Colliery' at the time of this disaster, but only one, the Coppull Hall Colliery, was used for raising the coal. The furnace pit, named the Coppull Pit, was about 640 yards away, due north from the Coppull Hall and, incredibly, the ventilation here was still achieved by hanging a fire bucket in the shaft. Another pit, known as the Dry Bones shaft was used as a downcast, and was about the same distance away from the Coppull Hall Colliery, in a north-eastern direction.

The Burgh Pit, where the previous explosion took place, was still in existence, but worked out as far as coal getting was concerned, but then used in ventilation as a downcast pit and secondary access.

The Coppull Hall Colliery, also known as the New Pit, was sunk soon after the first explosion of 1846; whether this was done to improve the ventilation or not, or simply to access another area of coal we will now never know. The shaft at the New Pit was sunk to a depth of 210 yards, and from the bottom of this shaft a tunnel was driven to connect with the Coppull Pit, where the ventilation fire was located, thus effecting a ventilation circuit. About 280 yards along this tunnel was a level roadway driven in to the coal seam, and another one 40 yards further on, followed by a third at the same distance. It was in these tunnels that the work of actually extracting the coal was done. At the time of the disaster, the coal had been worked in these tunnels for a distance of 100 yards, and the colliers were now working their way back, taking the pillars of coal left to support the roof through the previous operations. Altogether around 140 men and boys were employed underground, ninety of them working in the place where the explosion occurred.

On the morning of Thursday 20 May 1852, the fireman at the pit, Thomas Smith, went down the shaft of the Coppull Hall Colliery around twenty minutes to five in the morning to make his inspection, as was required by the rules. The men soon followed, but were ordered to stay at the head of the first of the tunnels where the coal was being worked, until fireman Smith returned to say that all was safe. On

The only map evidence of the former Coppull Colliery is on the local OS extract for 1844–48. Courtesy of the Ordnance Survey

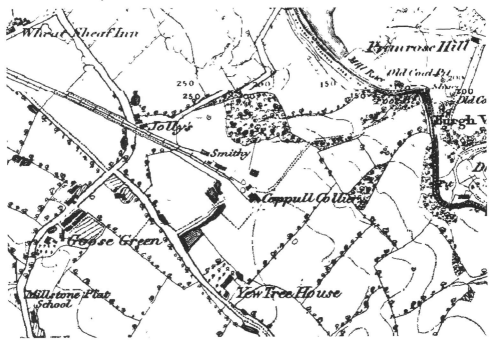

this day, the fireman, while making his inspection, came across a roof fall near to where the men would be working. The fall was up to the roof and had effectively stopped all the ventilation in this portion of the mine. Testing for gas with his Davy lamp, the fireman found that a large accumulation of methane gas had filled these workings. Returning to the main airway, he found that two men had gone down one of the other tunnels, and begun to start work in spite of what they had been told. The fireman ordered them out, telling them there was great danger and gas. He then told his fifteen-year-old son to stand guard at the spot and not let anyone past under any circumstances. Fireman Smith then went to continue his inspection of the rest of the workings and when he returned his son told him that two men had gone into the workings where the gas was, in spite of being told of the danger. Smith set off for the pit bottom to inform John Ellis, the son of the manager, and also an underlooker at the pit, of the danger. Ellis approved of what the fireman had done, and asked him to return to where the roof-fall had occurred, and to try make a clearing over the top in order to restore some sort of ventilation to rid the gas. Ellis said he would go and stop any of the men who had gone into the gas-ridden workings, and then each set off on their tasks.

They were going about this work, when at two minutes before seven, an explosion occurred. Those on the surface of the mine saw a fearful rush of dust-laden air shoot up the shaft skywards. Fully aware of what had happened under-ground, the cage was lowered, and a number of men and boys were drawn to the surface. By eight o'clock, around ninety had reached the surface, some of them effected by the afterdamp, and a number burnt to one extent or another. It was reckoned that about forty-odd more men and boys were still below ground, and efforts were then begun to rescue them. There was no lack of volunteers, and soon the cage was lowered again, this time with a searching party. The air was found to be breathable as far as the tunnels, which went into the area where the coal was being worked, but beyond here it was thick with the afterdamp. But still the rescuers struggled on. By ten o'clock three of their companions had been found dead. Between then and one o'clock, eighteen dead bodies had been removed from the pit. It was to be five o'clock that afternoon, before it could be said that all those left in the mine were out, and all of these were numbered among the total killed, thirty-two men and boys. Four others were to die from their injuries, making a total of thirty-six fatalities.

Nearly all those who perished were found in the area near the roof fall, and were suffocated by the afterdamp, or caught by the explosion itself while making their way out of the pit after having been warned of the danger. The first reports of those killed, were listed as:

William Ainscough, aged 36, of Coppull, who left a wife and two children
James Almond, aged 22, of Chorley
Thomas Banks, aged 40, of Coppull, who left a widow and three children
Robert Banks, aged 16, son of the above
Thomas Banks, aged 14, brother to the above, and son of James
William Baxendale, aged 29, of Coppull, who left a wife and three children
Ellis Berry, aged 28, of Chorley, who left a wife and one child
William Blackhurst, aged 23, of Duxbury

Richard Booth, aged 31, of Duxbury, who left a widow and two children
John Bradley, aged 26, of Coppull, who left a widow and two children
John Butterworth, aged 12, of Coppull
William Culshaw, aged 30, of Coppull
Henry Culshaw, aged 17, brother to the above
William Darbyshire, aged 35, of Duxbury, who left a widow and two children
James Darbyshire, aged 15, son of the above
John Ellis, aged 24, of Coppull, underlooker, son of the manager
William Green, aged 30, of Chorley, who left a widow and three children
Richard Green, aged 27, of Chorley, brother of the above, who left a widow and child
Thomas Gregson, aged 40, of Coppull, who left a widow and four children
John Gregson, aged 9, son of the above
George Howarth, a lad of Chorley
Thomas Miller, aged 20 of Chorley
Peter Moorfield, aged 25, of Coppull, who left a widow and two children
William Morris, aged 31, of Duxbury, who left a widow and five children
Edward Robinson, aged 30, of Coppull, who left a widow and child
John Roscow, aged 24, of Coppull
William Ryding, aged 21, of Coppull
Robert Smith, aged 17, of Coppull, son of the fireman
Thomas Southworth, aged 12, of Chorley
Robert Tootal, aged 13, of Coppull
Stephen Turner, aged 30, of Wrightington, who left a widow and two children
James Turner, aged 41, of Coppull, who left a widow and four children
Thomas Watson aged 40, of Coppull, widower with four children

Besides the thirty-three listed as dead above, a further six were classed as 'seriously injured'. They were:

John Culshaw, aged 25, brother of the two listed as dead above
Henry Dickenson, aged 45, of Chorley, a widower
John Farrington, aged 20, of Coppull
Samuel Holcroft, aged 25, of Coppull
James Hunter, aged 18, of Coppull
John Yates, aged 27, of Chorley, who left a widow and two children

Samuel Holcroft, listed above, died the Saturday following the explosion; John Yates died on the Sunday, and John Farrington on the Monday. This brought the total killed at the Coppull Hall Colliery to thirty-six. The inquest into the disaster was held in the *Royal Oak Hotel* at Chorley before Mr Palmer, coroner for the Leyland Hundred. Mr Dickinson, the Inspector of Mines for the area, was also present, and critical of the whole affair of the colliery management. After hearing all the evidence, the jury returned a verdict of *Accidental death* with the following provisos. The jury thought that the proprietor, might with very good results provide lamps for the men, and see that they were properly used on all occasions. In particular, forcing every man to take a lamp down the pit with him, and for use in case the workings became dangerous, although it might be considered safe to allow candles to be generally used in some of the workings. Mr Hargreaves (the owner) said that, not being a practical collier, he relied on those he consulted. He had been advised that the Davy lamp could not be used for general purposes, although to some extent it was very useful. But for this he would have enforced the regular use of the lamp four or five years since, when the explosion occurred in one of the other pits connected with the colliery. He had acted on the advice of his general manager, Mr Ellis and his surveyor, their opinion, being confirmed by that of another surveyor not connected with the colliery. He said that he would readily adopt anything which would tend to secure the safety of the men. He would supply lamps and enforce their use, if he could be shown it would be practicable. He had never allowed expense to be an obstacle in carrying out what he had been advised. With that the inquiry concluded, at the same time as news was coming in of another explosion at the colliery the previous day. It appeared that a boy named Booth had gone into some old workings at the pit with a naked light. An explosion followed immediately, burning the boy, along with a man named James Bannister, and two other boys named William Cooper and Joseph Turner, the latter three seriously. One might wonder just what it would take to enforce the use of Davy lamps and ban candles altogether in such a dangerous mine!

Later, Coppull Colliery changed hands, but the improvements did not change the situation. The *Colliery Guardian* reported on 30 December 1865, that T R Bourne, owner of the Coppull Hall Colliery, near Chorley, had been charged with having only one shaft, and employing more than twenty men in the pit at the time, contrary to the Mines Act; also for not having sufficient ventilation at the pit, when a man named Richard Marsden was killed in the mine through an excess of gas. He was fined £15. A lasting reminder of the events of 20 May 1853, can be seen at the parish church at Coppull. On the right-hand side when entering the churchyard is the memorial to John Ellis, the son of the manager who perished at the New Pit, Coppull Hall Colliery. The forty-four others who died in the horrific explosions at the Coppull Colliery all those years ago are denied mention, including the girls and the young lads, one aged just seven years old, surely a situation which can now be altered! It would not cost a great deal of money to have a simple memorial to these sad and important events in Coppull's historic past. The dead children, and the miners who perished in the explosions at the Coppull deserve that at least.

Part Two
The Era of Frequent Disasters
1853–1870

(8) Ince Hall & Cannel Company, Arley Mine: 24th March 1853

As the perished were brought out of the mine they were conveyed on carts to the Navigation Inn ...

The Ince Hall & Cannel Company's Arley Mine was located to the east of Britannia Bridge off Warrington Lane to the south of Wigan, and between locks numbers 16 and 18 on the Leeds & Liverpool Canal. As with most old colliery sites, the place today is taken over by playing fields, situated between Britannia Bridge and The Grove. Other pits belonging to the same company lay across Ince Moss to the east. The Arley Mine formed just two pits of a cluster from no less than eight coal pits belonging to the company. The Arley Mine, with its two shafts, was sunk to a depth of about 414 yards, and in 1853 had only been at work for about three years. In charge of the cluster of mines belonging to the Ince Hall and Cannel Company's pits was James Darlington, brought down from the North East, due to his great mining experience. Under Darlington, and in charge of the surface running of the Arley Mines, was George Bury. Below ground here, the works were the responsibity of Thomas Jones. In opening up the Arley Mine, the company chose to drive the tunnels on all four points of the compass to the boundary, almost a mile at one point, and then retreat the work by extracting the coal back towards the shafts. This was a system of mining adopted much later by the National Coal Board. It is an expensive system, as no return is gained until the actual work of taking the coal is begun, but it did have advantages. One of these is that, once completed, no time was wasted in making the roadways and ventilation circuits (these having been done previously) and all the work involved was that of the main function of a colliery, that of taking the coal.

The coal-winding shaft at the Arley Mines, was also the upcast shaft, where a furnace placed at the bottom of the pit effected the ventilation. On Wednesday morning, 24 March 1853, between 140 and 150 men and boys descended the downcast shaft at the Arley Mine to start their day's work. During the morning, the cage at the upcast shaft jammed on a number of occasions in the shaft. This fault was due to one of the guide rods, which guided the cages in the pit shaft, keeping them away from the walls of the shaft. The underlooker, Thomas Jones, stopped the winding of coal, and ordered that the fire at the ventilation furnace be damped down, reducing the current through the mine so that the matter could be attended to. The fumes from the furnace of course, and all the 'foul' and gas would have been drawn to the surface, and hindered the work. This then enabled the joiners at the pit to descend the shaft and carry out repair works to the guide rods. Jones envisaged that the work would only take an hour, or an hour and a half at most, and therefore did this work without consultation with the general manager of the works, James Darlington.

When the repairs had been carried out, Jones ordered that the furnace be fired up again to full strength. Wednesday was also the fortnightly pay-day for the men employed at the pit, so they were all keen to get out of the mine. By around twelve o'clock upwards of sixty-four men had been raised at the upcast, with another twenty or so remaining at the shaft bottom. A few minutes after one o'clock, the pit 'fired' and searing yellow flames vented up the shaft, tearing away the iron

An early view of the Ince Hall and Cannel Company's Arley Mine. From the Illustrated London News, *9 April 1853.* www.cmhrc.co.uk

landing plates at the surface. It was not a loud explosion, but it did shake the earth, and rattled the furniture of two public houses, the *Britannia*, and the *Navigation* at the Canal Bridge, almost 300 yards away. Dirt, dust and debris was forced up the pit and hurled into the air, some of it landing in the canal. The upcast shaft where the furnace was situated, was considerably damaged in the blast, the cage destroyed, and the guide rods torn from their mountings on the shaft walls. Hot yellow sulphurous fumes and thick dark smoke poured up from the dark working of the pit. It was impossible to descend the upcast shaft, now severely damaged – in any case, in all but the rarest of occasions would the upcast shaft have been used for any rescue attempt. The afterdamp would have been at its thickest at this shaft, and any smoke from fires below would also have risen here. The general manager, James Darlington, was just coming out of his office, when the pit fired. He noticed the smoke and the ventilation reversed for about two minutes, before restoring itself. A man of Darlington's experience was soon aware of what had happened, and immediately began to organise the colliers on the surface. The pit bank almost immediately became the gathering ground of anxious relatives and womenfolk, hoping and praying for news of loved ones.

Darlington ordered water from the nearby canal to be poured down the down-cast shaft of the pit, to try and restore some of the ventilation current. This continued for around fifteen or twenty minutes, by which time he had an exploration party ready to descend the pit by way of the downcast shaft. The party in the cage included Mr Darlington, Thomas Jones, the underlooker of the Arley Mines, and four or five working colliers. The cage was lowered into the depths of the pit but, before reaching the bottom, the order was given to raise the exploratory party up the shaft since the afterdamp was too thick to support life. Water was ordered to be thrown down the shaft and this continued for another half hour, before another attempt could be made into the workings. The afterdamp was still strong at the bottom of the pit but, through extreme brave attempts, the party struggled onwards and managed to reach the ventilation furnace. Strong wooden doors separating the two shafts had been blown to atoms in the fury of the explosion. A signal was received from below to those on the surface and, amazingly, eight to ten men, uninjured apart from suffering from the afterdamp, were raised to the pit bank. All of them were weak from the effects of the poisonous fumes, and had to be carried out of the cage in groups, between two of the surface workers, the young lads were conveyed out on the backs of older men.

These fortunate survivors were taken to a nearby engine house, where brandy and other stimulants were administered, after which they either walked home, or were sent there in cabs. The crowds gathered in ever larger numbers on the pit bank to await news from below, apprehensively waiting to hear news of their husbands, brothers, or fathers. The scenes of sobbing and mourning became heart rendering but all remained calm. Blackening clouds and relentless rains only added to the gloom of the day, and the catastrophe that was slowly unveiling itself. Bricks and timber were ordered to be sent down into the pit, to repair the ventilation doors damaged in the blast, and to restore the air current vital for life. In a short time, another five men and boys were raised, all in a very exhausted condition; one of these, Aaron Jelly, also suffered a fractured skull and leg. By half-past five that afternoon, the number of men and boys raised from the underground hell numbered twenty-five, all alive, but suffering to one extent or another from the afterdamp. The crowd on the surface by this time had grown so large that it was deemed more prudent that those who failed to survive should be recovered and remain at the shaft bottom until the crowd diminished, or at least lessened in numbers. As darkness drew in, the grieving crowds slowly drifted away, save for a few and, at about a quarter to midnight, the first of the dead men and boys were raised to the surface. As the perished were brought out of the mine they were conveyed on carts to the *Navigation Inn* between the pit and Wigan town. Here, they were placed in two barns on a bed of straw, where they remained to be viewed by the coroner's jury following the opening of the inquest.

Below ground, fifty-odd men, headed by Mr Darlington, still struggled on to restore the air circuit, and continued to find those still in the mine, dead or alive. Remarkably, one man was found alive, at around half past three on Thursday morning His name was Robert Williams and he was in the furthest part of the workings, three quarters of a mile from the pit bottom.

The inquest into the disaster was fixed for one o'clock the following day, being Good Friday, at the *Navigation Inn*. The grimmest of tasks came first, to view the bodies of the deceased men and boys in the outbuilding of the inn. It now remained to catalogue those who had died at the Arley Mine that day. It was indeed a disaster in every sense, with fifty-eight men and boys, some as young as eleven years of age, killed in the blast. It is clear that many were related since brothers, fathers and sons were listed as victims of the catastrophe. At last, it was possible to name those who died:

John Mardsen, aged 33, hooker-on, of Wigan, married with two children.

John Stanley, aged 21, hooker-on, of Wigan, unmarried

Joseph Hunt, aged 37, fireman, married with six children

Edward Hunt, aged 15, a drawer, son of Joseph named above

Michael Connelly, aged 21, a jigger, of Wigan, unmarried

James Green, aged 11, a drawer, of Wigan

Richard Bannister, aged 30, collier, of Chorley, married with five children

William Taberner, aged 20, labourer, of Ince, unmarried

Joseph Taberner, aged 18, jigger, of Ince, brother of William above, unmarried

Joseph Blacklidge, a boy, drawer, of Chorley

George Hargreaves, aged 24 or 25, drawer, of Wigan, married with two children

William McKnight, aged 25, jigger, of Wigan, married with one or two children

Thomas Baxendale, aged 38, of Wigan, a labourer, married with two children

William Gent, aged 19 of Wigan, a drawer, unmarried

Samuel Gent, aged 20, drawer, brother to William above, unmarried

Eli Jelly, aged 34 or 35, collier, of Wigan, unmarried

Thomas Wright, aged 35, collier, of Wigan, married with five children

William Byrom, aged 26, collier, of Wigan, unmarried

Matthew Rigby, aged 23, collier, of Wigan, unmarried

John Huyton, aged about 52, labourer, of Wigan, married with six or seven children

John Mellin aged 20, drawer, of Wigan, unmarried

James Jones, aged 18, jigger, of Ince, unmarried

John M'Allister, aged 20, a drawer, of Wigan

James M'Allister, aged 14, drawer, of Wigan

Joseph McAllister, aged 16, drawer, of Wigan, all brothers

Henry Isherwood, aged 27, drawer, of Wigan, married with one child

Edward Marsden, aged 18, drawer, of Wigan

Joseph McIntosh, aged 29, collier, of Wigan, married with two children

Peter McNaught, aged 15, drawer, of Wigan

Robert McNaught, aged 13, drawer, brother of the above, of Wigan

Edward Hanley, aged 12, drawer, of Wigan

John Cavanagh, aged 22, drawer, of Wigan, married with one child

Michael Cunliffe, aged 22 or 23, a jigger, of Wigan

Matthew Byrnes, aged 21, drawer, of Wigan

Robert Jones, aged 26, collier, of Wigan, married with three children

Thomas Ellison, aged 20, collier, of Wigan, unmarried

Robert Lewis, aged 22, collier, of Wigan, married, no children

James Harrison, aged 45, horse-tenter & furnace-man, of Wigan, married with six children

Ralph Valentine, aged 25, labourer, of Wigan, married with one child

Cutus Morgan, aged 18, collier, of Wigan, unmarried

Thomas Owen, aged 30, collier, of Wigan, married with two children

James Hardman, aged 13, door-tenter, of Ince

Joseph Gaskell, aged 20, collier, of Wigan, unmarried

William Griffiths, aged 32, collier, of Ince, unmarried

Charles O'Neill, aged 28, collier, of Ince, unmarried

Arthur O'Neill, aged 21, collier, of Ince, brother to the above, unmarried

John O'Neill, aged 18, drawer, brother to the two above, unmarried

Thomas Glaive, aged 22, collier, of Wigan, unmarried

John Davies, a 'young man', drawer, of Ince, unmarried

Thomas Jones [no details]
David Jones [no details]

The above list, taken from first reports on the explosion, only lists fifty-one victims. The other seven of the total fifty-eight who officially died are presumed to have included a number of the injured identified below:

Robert Ainscough, aged 28, collier, of Wigan, dangerously injured
James Naylor, aged 26, collier, of Wigan, injured by the afterdamp
William Ainscough, aged 13, jig-tenter, of Wigan, slightly injured by the afterdamp
William Critchley, a 'young man', of Wigan, seriously injured
An 'unnamed boy' of Wigan, fractured leg, and much 'blown'
Aaron Jelly, of Wigan, fractured leg and skull
Thomas Martindale, arm fractured, and other injuries
A man named Mason, hurt on the back etc.

So what did cause this terrible colliery disaster? Was it, as some thought, brought about by the accumulation of gas through damping down the furnace? Or was there some other cause? The pits were reported to have been worked on the strictest of terms – on no account whatsoever were the men and boys allowed to take candles below ground. All the men were supplied with locked safety lamps, and there were severe penalties for opening them underground. Yet notwithstanding these regulations, such was the disregard by the colliers themselves, in as much that the rules were still broken. On the day before this great disaster, one of the colliers in the Cannel Mine belonging to the same company took down some cloth erected near his work for the purpose of ventilation. The following day, the day of the disaster, he entered the place with his Davy lamp, and had by some means picked the lock, thus exposing the naked flame of the lamp. An explosion followed immediately whereby the man was seriously burnt. The adjourned inquest into the tragedy at the Arley Mine was resumed in the National School at Ince Green the following Thursday before adjourning further. The inquiry ended on Saturday 9 April 1853, when the jury returned the following verdict:

We find that the death of Edward Marsden and fifty six others, whose bodies we have viewed, was caused by an explosion of firedamp, which occurred on the 23 March last, in the Arley Pit, situated at Ince, belonging to the Ince Hall Coal and Cannel Company, and that the explosion occurred from gas which accumulated in No. 6 drift, and other drifts on the south side of the No. 2 north jigger. There is no direct evidence to show how such gas ignited, or how the accumulation took place. But the jury are of the opinion that it arose from a door on the south side of No. 2 north jigger being improperly left open for a longer or shorter period. The jury cannot separate without strongly expressing their opinion that the rules for the said colliery are very imperfectly carried into execution.

A damming verdict however you look at it, which gives little consideration to those who had actually perished – just another mining disaster. The doors mentioned, are termed air-doors, and when working properly should remain closed at all times, save for the passing of men and materials. They control the flowing air current through the mine and prevent any short-circuiting of the air and accumulation of gasses. The coroner then thanked the jury, and the proceedings were ended, having occupied upwards of four full days in total.

(9) Bardsley Colliery: 2 February 1858

As the rescue workers neared the upcast shaft, they saw, to their horror, that a portion of the wood lining of the shaft was on fire ...

The Bardsley Colliery was one of some antiquity, it being mentioned in the Reports on Child Labour in the Coal Mines, 1841, when it was worked by the Harrop family of Bardsley. The pit was located in village of Bardsley, around mid-way between Oldham and Ashton-under-Lyne, and on the Oldham side of 'Bardsley Bridge'. There were once numerous other pits at work in this area. These included, at various dates, the Woodpark, Limehurst, Rocher and pits around Fairbottom Bobs. Most locals will remember the Woodpark Colliery which closed down in the mid-1950s.

There were two shafts at the Bardsley Colliery. The one nearest to Ashton-under-Lyne, known as the Diamond Pit, was the downcast shaft, and was also used for the ascent and descent of the men, and sunk to a depth of 500 yards. The other pit was called the Victoria Pit, an indication of just when it was sunk, and was situated around 100 yards north of the former. This pit (the Victoria) was the upcast, or furnace pit, but also used for winding the coal, and was 490 yards deep. From the bottom of the 'Diamond Shaft', the downcast shaft, a tunnel named the 'gin brow' was driven a distance of 500 yards to the south. Two tunnel levels were then driven off the 'gin brow' to the boundary of the mine to the west, a total distance of 500 yards. To the east of the 'gin brow' was another level tunnel of 300 yards to the working coal faces.

Two seams of coal were worked at the Bardsley Colliery, the lowest being the Peacock Mine, and the other one, around 20 feet above, was known as the Two Feet Mine. Around 1856, the colliery passed from the Harrops to the Bardsley Colliery Company. Under this company, a furnace ventilation system was installed. Prior to this the air-flow through the pit was achieved by the outdated method of having a fire lowered into the upcast shaft. The colliery was a major employer for Bardsley village. On Tuesday 2 February 1858, 183 men and boys descended the pit shaft at the Bardsley Pit. About seventy of these were colliers, the rest young men and boys employed as drawers, or waggoners. The day's work progressed normally and without incident, and by half-past four and five o'clock in the afternoon, about half the number employed below ground, mainly the colliers had finished their work, were on the surface or making their way out of the pit. Those still below were the younger lads, the drawers, and about a dozen of them were at the bottom of the shaft 'hooking on' or sending up the shaft the loaded tubs of coal.

At ten minutes past five, the tiny mining village of Bardsley was shaken by a deafening report. All eyes turned to the colliery, their deepest fears were realised, when locals found out that the pit had indeed exploded. Volumes of black smoke and dust flew from the upcast shaft at the pit, confirmation, were it needed, that the pit had fired. Only mining communities can share the grief that followed, the women, mothers, daughters, wives, and sisters, rushed to the pit bank for news of their cherished ones still below ground. As in all colliery disasters, there was no lack of volunteers, the overlookers, underlookers, colliers, young drawers; and many from the other coal mines close at hand, who themselves had just finished their labours, were instantly on the Bardsley pit bank. In no other industry other than mining, would men and boys launch themselves with perhaps forlorn hope into a potentially lethal environment to save their fellow workers, their comrades and friends and to get those beyond help out of the smoking pit. As the thick fumes and smoke continued to pour from the shaft any descent into the mine was fraught with fears of another explosion. Under the direction of Mr Whitehead, the principal viewer at the Bardsley Colliery, the necessary rescue operations were initiated. At the downcast shaft, the winding ropes had been blown off the head-stocks, and the cage itself damaged by the force of the explosion. At the upcast shaft, the damage was to a much lesser extent, but this was of little importance so the searchers had to work from the downcast shaft. Any poisonous gases from the workings would be coming up through the upcast shaft, and in this respect this shaft was useless as far as rescue work was concerned. As quickly as possible repairs were made to the downcast shaft and the cage there. The cage was lowered into the mine where it was known, from cries below, that a number of men had been waiting at the bottom. Some of these were found beyond help, others were disabled or injured to some degree or other, and thirty of these were brought to the pit bank in quick succession.

Two hours after the explosion, the first of the search parties was able to descend into the still smoking and fume-filled underground galleries. Making their way slowly through the blackness, smoke and damaged workings they came across eight or ten men and boys who were lying dead as the searchers neared the upcast shaft underground. As the rescuers neared the upcast shaft, they saw to their horror that a portion of the wood lining of the shaft was on fire, as was a portion of the coal seam close by. While this fire continued, there was no question of restoring the ventilation, so vital to life, and the rescue attempts had to be quickly aborted. There was a very real and immediate danger that any explosive gases coming into contact with the fire would result in further underground blasts. Efforts were thus confined to putting out the fires, with scores of men and boys employed throwing down buckets of water into the pit, and a steam jet was used to provide a safer alternative ventilation. It was not however until two o'clock the following Wednesday morning that the fires were finally extinguished, when the rescue parties then were able to exert themselves to the job in hand: to get the injured and dead out of the mine. Even so, the workings were still filled with the deadly afterdamp, and the searchers could only work in one-hour shifts, each eagerly being replaced by another team, as they emerged exhausted from the fume-filled pit. By eight o'clock on the Wednesday morning upwards of twenty-five dead men and boys had been raised from below; but it was believed that same number, or even more, might still be in the pit. In the confusion of the events, men and boys had been raised before the blast, others had been raised after the explosion, and rushed to medical aid, while others had simply gone home, or were involved in the rescue. No-one it seemed knew who was in or out of the pit, who had gone home, who had been injured, who was safe, or who was dead.

Many of the dead victims at the Bardsey Colliery were conveyed to their own homes before being laid to rest. This Victorian print, reproduced from the illustrated London News, *typifies the scene.*
www.cmhrc.co.uk

It was decided to take a roll call; the total number known to have been in the pit at the start of the day when the explosion occurred was put at 183. Those known to have perished was put at twenty-eight, another fourteen were thought to still be in the pit with little chance of having survived. Thirty-two others had been burned or otherwise injured, and some of these later succumbed to their injuries. The rest were all safe, having been raised before the blast. Those who had perished were taken to the *Horse Shoe* public house to be viewed at the coroner's inquest, before being released for burial. The list made up a sickening account of life snuffed out of existence, many of them young lads, employed as drawers. The first accounts gave the following names:

Known to be dead

George Turner, lying at the *Horse Shoe*, married

John Bredbury, of Waterloo, brought out alive, but died soon after

Forrester Brierley, of Bardsley, a boy

Jonah Taylor, of Ashton-under-Lyne, a boy

Samuel Taylor, lying at the *Horse Shoe*, who left a widow and several children

Joseph Taylor, lying at the *Horse Shoe*, son of the above

Edward Taylor, lying at the *Horse Shoe*, also son of Samuel above

Joseph Lomas, lying at the *Horse Shoe*, a boy

John Brierley, of Bardsley, a boy

Ralph Matley of Bardsley, a boy, son of one of the firemen

William Quarmby of Bardsley, a boy

Isaiah Ingham of Bardsley, who was married left a widow and one or two children

John Roberts of Bardsley, who left a widow and five children

William Yardley of Bardsley, a boy

Joseph Barber of Smallshaw, who was married, but family unknown

Peter Knight of Oldham, who was married but family unknown, he was carried home, but died in two hours

James Lees, of Bardsley, a boy

Thomas Robinson, left a widow and two of three children

Thomas Stafford, of Bardsley, who was married with two or three children

James ———— (a stranger), lying at the *Horse Shoe*

Joseph Bancroft of Bardsley, who was married, family unknown

Jonathan Wardle, one of the firemen of Bardsley, left a wife and two or three children

William Ibbetson, lying at the *Horse Shoe*, married

George Ibbetson, lying at the *Horse Shoe*, brother of the above

James Stringer of Bardsley, a widower with four children

Samuel Ogden of Bardsley

Thomas Cooper

Samuel Hampson of Bardsley, unmarried

The bodies of those not stated to be at the *Horse Shoe*, were conveyed to their late homes, or the homes of their parents in Bardsley, or neighbouring villages. Joseph Bancroft, listed above, was 'frightfully shattered'. He was with others standing at the opening to the Two Foot seam waiting for the cage. The force of the explosion forced them into the shaft and dashed him and the others against the sides of the pit. They then fell a distance of around 30 to 40 feet into the sump hole at the bottom. Many of the bodies found to be dead were 'blackened' or otherwise injured from the fierce heat and burning effects of the explosion.

Believed to be in the pit dead were:

Robert Davies

Thomas Rigby

David Evans

James Winterbottom

Robert Hyde

Joseph Hall
Abraham Wordall
Samuel Leach
Joseph Wright
John Schofield
Peter Dunn (a lad)
John Clark
Edmund Bredbury
One man unnamed

The above list only names forty-two men and boys as having perished in the disaster but the Mines Inspectors' Report for the year gives the number who died at the Bardsley Colliery that day as fifty-three. It is assumed that those named as being 'burnt or otherwise injured' died later, namely:

James Davies
Peter Howarth
–?– Moors
–?– Pickup
John Greaves
James Taylor
Henry Rutcliffe
Henry Cooper
William Cooper, all severely [injured]
John Davies
–?– Davies, son of the above
James Hopkins, Daniel Cavanagh, severely [injured]
John Hewitt, dangerously ill
Joseph Yardley, very severely [injured]
William Ibbetson, severely [injured]
John Rigby
David Dawson
–?– Hopkins
–?– Howarth
Thomas Cooper, John Shaw, both very serious
Thomas Shaw, very serious
Thomas Jones, Samuel Stepney, James Simpson, severely [injured]
David Robinson, Thomas Bentham, Andrew Lees, Samuel Robinson, severely [injured]
Isaac Parry, very serious.

By the time the inquest had come to its verdict, the number of dead men and boys was put at fifty-two. The verdict of the inquest was as follows:

We the jury are of the unanimous opinion that the explosion was accidentally caused by blasting in the No.1 Level, south of the gin brow in the Two Feet Mine, and was thence communicated to the other parts of the pit.

The Foreman then read the following recommendations, as agreed by the jury:

(1) Owing to the fiery nature of these mines, the jury recommend that blasting with gunpowder be entirely discontinued.

(2) They consider the ventilation of the more remote parts of the workings insufficient, and recommend improved air passages therein, together with such additional alterations as may secure this object.

(3) They are further of the opinion that greatly increased vigilance and care are absolutely necessary in working these mines, and in order to secure this object, they strongly urge the employment of under-viewers of greater intelligence and scientific attainments.

There is by all accounts a memorial (or at least a mass grave) to the victims of an explosion at the Bardsley Colliery in the nearby churchyard according to a local I spoke to. Whether this is the explosion of 1858 I was unable to define, as at the time the church was undergoing extensive renovation. Certainly, there was no greater disaster at Bardsley. It would be nice however, if this is the reminder of the disaster, that it be uncovered, and perhaps even restored, in remembrance of the appalling events of 2 February 1858. The men and boys who died that day paid the ultimate cost, and we should not forget them, or the price they paid. Mining continued at the Bardsley Colliery, until the pit was finally abandoned in 1884. The events of 1858, just twenty-six year before, would beyond doubt still have been forever haunting those who lost loved ones in this appalling mining disaster. Bardsley village continued to live under the dark cloud of such potential danger to their loved ones, until the nearby Woodpark Colliery was abandoned in March 1955, ending coal mining at Bardsley for ever. There are few remains of this former industry today at Bardsley village. Coal Pit Lane survives, besides the site of what used to be the Woodpark Colliery and, depicting a colliery headgear and pit tubs on its inn sign, is the *Black Diamond*. Black Diamonds they may have been, but the diamonds were mined at a dreadful human cost.

(10) Tyldesley Colliery: 13 December 1858

Two young brothers named Beswick were found closely embraced in each other's arms, as if asleep, suffocated by the afterdamp.

The Yew Tree Pit was part of the Tyldesley Colliery workings, situated east of the railway station at Tyldesley and north of the Manchester Road just beyond Milk Street, not far from the town hall. The site today is probably that taken to the north of the Central Primary School at Tyldesley, or at least close by. The pit was worked by Messrs Green and Holland, and the shaft was 250 yards deep. The underground workings at the pit extended a considerable distance in 1858, going under St George's Church, some 1,100 yards away from the pit mouth, although it was stated that 'the colliery is not of very long standing' implying that the pit was quite new. On the morning of 13 December 1858, the men and boys descended the pit as was normal when, around eleven o'clock a number of the men noticed that the air was very bad, gas laden and noxious; indeed, some of these men decided that it was time to get out of the workings. At around twelve noon, the pit exploded. Unlike most pit explosions, there was no loud blast to reveal itself at the shaft; in fact by all accounts the actual explosion was minimal, and most of those who perished did so in the deadly afterdamp. This is the lethal gas left behind following an explosion, when all the oxygen has been used up by the flames of the blast. The afterdamp's effects are suffocation, collapse, then death and there is little chance of escape in the confines of the restricted airways and tunnels of a coal mine.

Following the explosion, the Yew Tree Pit was fully charged with afterdamp, which was slow to clear. So poor was the ventilation at the pit, that all attempts to enter the workings by rescue workers were thwarted by the afterdamp for at least two or three hours after the initial explosion. By four o'clock, and with considerable effort, the rescue teams, aided by management and workers from other local collieries, had traversed a considerable distance, to a point known as the 'jig brow'. But in spite of all these efforts, they only succeeded in finding one dead body. Between five and six o'clock, news was sent to the surface that another seven lifeless bodies had been found; and, in the opinion of the explorers, no one left in the gas filled workings could have survived. It was now just a case of recovering the dead, ending the struggle and forlorn hope of finding anyone alive. Large crowds, estimated by some as several thousand gathered for news at the pit head.

Orders were given that none of those who had perished should be brought to the surface until late at night, in the chance and hope that the assembled crowd would have diminished, thus avoiding the scenes of woe. At 10.17 pm the cage was wound slowly to the surface bringing up the first of the dead men and boys.

The scene at the pit-head on the day of the disaster at Tyldesley Colliery, from the Illustrated London News, *25 December 1858.* www.cmhrc.co.uk

As midnight approached, fifteen bodies had been removed from the pit, and with just one exception, that of a man named Hugh Aspinall, all others had succumbed to the suffocating effects of the afterdamp. It was assumed that Aspinall, realising the accumulation of methane gas was about to ignite, was running to warn others, when the explosion took place when his body was literally blown to pieces. Throughout the night the unabated efforts to reach those below continued. As the searchers moved forward deeper into the workings, their progress was confounded by considerable masses of wreckage, consisting of roof falls, broken timbers, and upturned tubs that slowed the recovery down. Strong and willing hands eagerly moved the tons of rubble and rock that barred the way to their unfortunate comrades; the men worked on with stupendous effort. By morning, the rescuers had found another three bodies, each so completely dismembered, that it was impossible to identify them. As these were returned to the surface, those that could be recognised were removed to their respective homes on carts, conveyed through the grieving crowds.

By noon the following day, twenty-four hours after the explosion, six men and boys were still unaccounted for and it was supposed that the total number of those who perished was twenty five. However, this was not the case, an error arose when one of the men's thighs, blown off in the blast, was discovered under some debris and mistaken for the trunk of a boy, but later the lad's body was recovered and identified. The total number, therefore, of men and boys who perished at the Yew Tree Pit that day was twenty-four. There were some pitiful tales, and courageous ones, from the hell below to be told. One poor fellow, a young lad well acquainted with the air courses in the pit, had partially succeeded in opening an air door, which would have taken him to a fresher atmosphere. Before he could complete his escape, the afterdamp overtook him, his body eventually found by the searchers. He was still clasping his pick. Two young brothers named Beswick were found closely embraced in each other's arms, as if asleep, suffocated by the afterdamp.

In another case, one sturdy collier in his escape took with him a considerable distance through the noxious atmosphere two youths, who had become insensible towards the shaft bottom. He was thoroughly exhausted by the time they were raised up, but all three survived. The inquest at a later date had some scathing attacks on the running of the mine, when they returned the following verdict:

Our verdict is accidental death. We cannot however, allow this opportunity to pass without expressing our unanimous opinion that due precautions have not been taken to ensure the lives of the workmen employed in the mine; finding that the ventilation of the mine has generally been imperfect, more especially from the area of the out-let airways being much too small. We are also of the opinion that there has been a great want of practical knowledge of the working of the mine on the part of the underlooker, and also that the firemen have neglected their duties.

Those who perished that terrible day at the Tyldesley Colliery's Yew Tree Pit, were named as:

James Barlow, collier, who was married
William Baxter, collier, married with two children
Matthew Owen, collier, married with four or five children
Hugh Aspinall, collier, married

Peter Nightingale, collier, married
John Eckersley, collier, married
Henry Hope, collier, married with three children
Thomas Beswick, fireman, married with six or seven children
James Aldred, collier, single
Thomas Hindley, drawer, single
Michael Beswick, drawer, single
William Beswick, drawer, single
Thomas O'Neil, drawer, single
Richard Bradshaw, drawer, single
William Coop, drawer, single
Joseph Lythgoe, collier, married
John Lee, drawer, single
Lawrence Gurney, collier, widower, with two or three young children
Benjamin Foulds, drawer, single
James Tyrer, collier, married with a family
William Unsworth, drawer, single
William Lomax, collier
David Blackledge, drawer, single
Moses Brooks, foreman, married

It can be seen from the above that many of those who died listed as 'drawers', would have been young lads in their early teens, and the two named Beswick were related as brothers, with perhaps Thomas Beswick as the father. It is not as if the management were not aware of the dangers at the Yew Tree Pit, since there was a previous explosion there in April 1852, which claimed the life of Thomas Fletcher and another un-named person. The cause of the 1858 disaster was never really ascertained. The miners all used flame safety lamps, but these were all found intact. Poor ventilation without doubt was a major factor in allowing the build up of gas – but how it came to be ignited there was no evidence to prove. By the mid-1890s, the Yew Tree Pits were being worked by the Tyldesley Coal Company Limited, and employed over 140 men and boys, but they appear to have been abandoned soon afterwards.

(11) Agecroft Colliery: 6 January, 1859

The cage creaked and groaned for a few seconds amidst the tangled steel, and then plunged down the pit shaft taking the unfortunate men and boys with it.

By far the greatest loss of life in large numbers in the coal mining communities of Lancashire, and other coalfields was caused by gas and coal dust explosions underground. Single accidents though, caused through roof falls, shaft and haulage incidents also took their toll. Shaft accidents involving cages, were possibly the second most cause of multiple deaths, after explosions, and in the early years of mining occurred with remarkable frequency. The shaft accident at the Agecroft Colliery, near Manchester was one such case, but by no means unique – there were many others.

Agecroft Colliery was one of Andrew Knowles and Sons pits, and dated from at least 1836, when a report stated that there was an explosion there seriously

One of the earliest views of Agecroft Colliery, from a postcard, c.1920. Peter Nadin collection

injuring a father and his son. The colliery was situated off the Agecroft Road, which runs off the Bolton Road, near Irlams O' Th' Height, Salford. The depth of the pits was about 360 yards, the winding engine of 120-horse power. The engine-house was located between the two shafts, and the engine worked the cages in both pits. As one cage went up, the other cage at the other shaft went down. The two shafts were 9 feet 6 inches in diameter, and 20 yards apart.

On Tuesday 6 January 1859, around half past seven in the morning, about twenty men descended the pit to start their day's work. The majority of the men employed at the pit had started a few days holiday, the Friday previous – hence the low number of men in the pit that day. A signal bell, which informed the engineer that the cage was within 60 yards of the surface, was fitted in the shaft. This signalling device was worked on a slide in the shaft and, as the cage passed, it clipped a weight, which was attached to a rope, which in turn rang the bell, warning the winder that the cage was nearing the top of the pit. Some work had been done on the signalling device the week before when the winding ropes had been shortened, due to stretching of the rope. Around fourteen loads of coal had been raised from the pit, and the signal had rung each time; and all appeared to be working as normal.

The twenty men below intended to finished work early in the morning, and at about nine-thirty, the surface foreman gave the all clear for the men below to be raised up the shaft, having stopped the coal winding. Three men and four boys entered the cage at the pit bottom and the engineer, Elias Booth (alias Turner), began to wind the cage up the pit. The cage was raised at speed and, to his horror, the engineer saw the cage wind past the top of the shaft. The banksman, the person in charge of the shaft top, called out 'Stop winding'. It was too late, the cage was drawn into the head gearing of the pit, 25 feet above the surface. The cage was fitted with a safety device, the 'Owen Catch', as at all Andrew Knowles and Sons collieries. This should detached the rope in situations such as this, and should have held it in a safe position, albeit suspended above the shaft.

However, because of the speed of the winding, the catch was drawn above the ends of the conductors on which they worked, so the safety device was rendered useless. The rope did become detached from the cage, but because the cage was now above the conductors, which should have held it, there was nothing to stop it falling back down the pit. The cage creaked and groaned for a few seconds amidst the tangled steel, and then plunged down the pit shaft taking the unfortunate men and boys with it. They were of course instantly killed. Some men still at the bottom realised what was happening, and rushed away from the shaft bottom to safety. When it was safe to approach, the poor suffers were found to be terribly mutilated, each having at least one broken limb; one had his head almost severed from the body, another through the force of the rapid descent had his shin bones thrust through the knees into his calves.

Those who died were named as:

Benjamin Tomlinson, collier, aged 60, who left a widow and several grown up children
James Green, collier, married with two children
William Latham, a miner aged 20 years, unmarried
Lastly, four boys: Thomas Lancaster, Thomas Edge, Luke Thomas and John Foster,
    their ages from 12 to 16 years

The bodies were brought up the pit and placed in coffins and taken to the *Packhorse Inn* at Irlams O' Th' Heights to await the inquest. After viewing the bodies of the deceased men and boys the following Thursday, and hearing all the evidence, the jury returned a verdict of 'Accidental death'.

Andrew Knowles and Sons Ltd began sinking two new shaft at the Agecroft Colliery, to be named Nos. 3 and 4 in about 1896. In January 1900, it was reported that the Trencherbone Seam at the new pits had been reached at a depth of 723 yards. The old pits, Nos. 1 and 2, continued to be worked from the Doe Seam, and in 1896 employed 371 men underground and 111 surface workers. The old pits however were allowed to fall into disuse, and on 11 June 1915 were abandoned and filled in. The new pit did not fair much better and closed in 1932. All the surface buildings were demolished, but the shafts remained. Between 1953–58, the National Coal Board began work on the site of the old colliery, and reusing the old Nos. 3 and 4 shafts reopened the pits to a depth of 590 yards. Another completely new shaft, No. 5, was sunk to a depth of 668 yards, being 24 feet in diameter. All the surface structures at the colliery, which many will remember, dated from this time. The old buildings of the original pit had been demolished during the 1930s. By 1985/86, 715 men were producing 519,000 tonnes from the Doe Seam at the mine, half the output going to the adjacent coal-fired power station. The Colliery closed and was demolished in 1991, and the site soon cleared. A commercial development company, Priority Sites, commenced construction of a £2 million industrial development on the site of the former Agecroft Colliery in Salford in December 2002, which, it is speculated, could facilitate the creation or safe-guarding of over ninety jobs in the area, but a fraction of the number of those employed at the former pit, but jobs nevertheless.

(12) Shevington Colliery, Prince Albert Pit: 1 November 1861

Not one of the dead men and boys were found at their working places, all had been trying to reach the shaft when they were struck down by the afterdamp.

Although named Shevington Colliery, the pit was actually some distance from the village of that name, and really nearer to Appley Bridge. The pit was off the Miles Lane, where to the north is Hullet Hall Farm, the colliery located just north of this. Numerous 'coal pits' were around this area during the 1840s, in fact during the construction of the M6 motorway to the west of the village of Shevington, no less than forty-three mineshafts were discovered. Today, none of the collieries or any evidence of them remain. The Shevington Colliery is listed in a directory of 1834, when Barlow and Son were working it, although at the time of this disaster John Tayleur and Son were working the pit. Mr Mackinson was the colliery manager at the time of this explosion, and the use of naked lights, or candles was permitted in the workings. The Prince Albert Pit of the Shevington Colliery was sunk to a depth of 260 yards.

There are no known images of Shevington Colliery but the OS map of 1844–48 shows the pit and its environs at that time. Courtesy of the Ordnance Survey

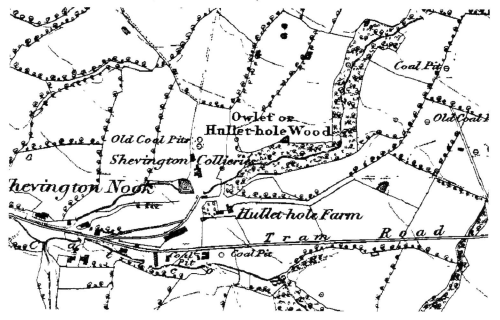

On the morning of Friday 1 November 1861, there were about twenty men employed in what was termed the 'south side workings'. At around half-past nine that morning, the men and boys heard a loud explosion, which was attributed to have happened nearer to the shaft than where they were working, and number of the men were scorched by the blast. The rest, fearing what had happened, and fully aware of the deadly consequences of the afterdamp, began to make their way to the shaft. Information was conveyed to the surface of the events underground, and a number of survivors were raised up the still smoking pit. Immediately, Mr Mackinson, and the fireman, Mr Close descended the pit. Heading the search party, they were soon pushing through towards the south side workings. A number of men were found, some unscathed, but others were dreadfully burnt by the searing heat of the explosion and those still alive were got out of the pit with all haste. On the surface they were greeted by a gathering crowd and provided with medical attention. As the search continued it was feared that no-one else could have survived the thick afterdamp that followed the blast, or that they had perished in the explosion itself – but still they searched. Soon, four dead bodies of their comrades were found at the start of the south side workings, but the afterdamp prevented further exploration. Work was concentrated on restoring the ventilation and ridding the pit of the deadly gases. By half-past three that afternoon, the searching was over – ten of their companions had perished, and another five were seriously injured. Not one of the dead men and boys were found at their working places. All had been trying to reach the shaft when they were struck down by the afterdamp.

A father in his haste to save his two sons took the wrong tunnel, and the gas suffocated all. Although ten were listed among the dead, three more were to die from their injuries, making a total of thirteen that perished in the Prince Albert Pit of the Shevington Colliery that day. The dead men and boys were:

William Crook, aged 59, a widower
James Ashcroft, aged 47, married
John Ashcroft, aged 15, son of the above
Solomon Ashcroft, aged 13, brother to the above, and son of James
Edward Goulden, aged 22, unmarried
James Baron, aged 12 years, a drawer
John Culshaw, aged 25
James Culshaw, aged 20, brother to John above
James Gaskell, aged 40, married with two children
William Yates, aged 40, unmarried

The injured, of whom three later died, were listed as:

William Riding, badly burnt
Robert Howcroft, very badly burnt about the head – died later
Ralph Ellison, face and arms burnt
Thomas Reed, burnt about the face and arms – died later
Robert Thompson, seriously burnt

There were also two ponies in the pit at the time of the explosion, and one of these was killed. There were pitiful scenes as the bodies were raised to the pit bank, the

This would have been a typical underground scene following a colliery explosion such as the one at Shevington, rescue workers crawling under or over roof falls and other hazards to reach colleagues. Miners knew no fear when the lives of their fellow workers were at stake since they knew that on another day it might be them waiting to be rescued. From the Illustrated London News, *28 September 1878.* www.cmhrc.co.uk

cries of bereaved mothers and wives was enough to melt the stoutest of hearts. The bodies themselves presented an appalling spectacle, some very badly burnt by the fierce heat of the explosion. To add further to the grief and heartache, was the death of Ann Reed, the wife of Thomas, named above as injured. She had been to Wigan market, where on her return, while still at the railway station, she was told of the explosion, and the injuries to her husband. The news affected her greatly and, as she neared the doorway of her house, she saw the surgeon's horse outside. Her daughter rushed indoors, and when she returned, her mother asked how her father was. She replied he was not badly hurt but the mother exclaimed that she knew otherwise, and that he would never recover. With that, the mother fell to the ground, and died within a few minutes.

The cause of the explosion that took away the thirteen lives that day was later attributed to the gas coming into contact with the open flame of the fireman named Riding, who was listed under the injured, but he is thought to have been the last to die from the explosion.

The Shevington Colliery was finally abandoned sometime before June 1877, and nothing remains today of the former pit that took away the lives of thirteen men and boys on that fateful day in November 1861. A tall chimney, however, at the pithead remained as a local landmark until as late as 1927. When that was finally removed by demolition, so too were the memories of the 1861 Shevington Colliery Disaster.

(13) Douglas Bank Colliery, 5 January 1865

... the foreman heard voices from under the tangled mess of bricks ...

Shaft sinking was a very highly skilled and specialised occupation but also extremely dangerous work, usually carried out by teams of men who moved around the country. There were various methods of sinking shafts, such as using steel tubing in water bearing strata, and later concrete. But the most common method was to line the shaft with a single course of brick. The shaft would be started off, and sunk to a depth of say 12 to 15 feet. Then, specially shaped wooden spars named curbing would be fastened to sidewalls at the bottom of the hole. The brickwork would then be built up to the surface, filling in any voids at the back with small rubble. The process would then be repeated downwards until the coal seam was reached. Shaft sinking could take anything from a year to several years depending on the strata, and final depth of the pit. Dangers in shaft sinking are very evident; those working at the bottom had little protection should anything fall down the pit. Their only option was to throw themselves to the side of the pit, and hope that whatever was falling missed them. There were, however, many deaths from this cause. Yet the accident at the Douglas Bank Colliery was very different, perhaps unique in Lancashire coal mining history.

The Douglas Bank Colliery was located near to the Pagefield Lock on the Leeds and Liverpool Canal, near Robin Park Stadium, Wigan. Sinking of the colliery started on 19 March 1863. There were to be two shafts at the pit, named the North Shaft and the South Shaft and, in the early days, a Furnace Shaft situated between the two main shafts achieved ventilation for the workings. The South Shaft was 16 feet in diameter, being the downcast and winding shaft. About 300 yards in a northerly direction was the North Shaft, also 16 feet in diameter and used for winding. The headgear at both shafts were built of pitch pine, and consisted of two main legs of 18-inch timber, and two upright legs for the shaft frame of 14-inch timber attached to the main pulley frame. The owners of the new pits were the Rose Bridge and Douglas Bank Colliery Company Ltd.

By January 1865, the shafts had reached and passed the Pemberton Five Feet, the Pemberton Four Feet, and were within yards of the Cannel Mine at a depth of 500 yards. Shortly before nine o'clock on Wednesday 5 January 1865, the shaft sinkers were busy at their work at the bottom of the pit, and had drilled some holes for blasting. They were then raised up the pit, and the shots were fired – everything appeared to be going as planned, and nothing out of the ordinary was envisaged. At ten minutes to nine o'clock, a party of eight men were lowered back into the pit in a hoppet, or large bucket, to remove the rubble caused by the blasting. The winding engineer was surprised to find that the hoppet, for no apparent reason, stopped suddenly in the shaft, a few yards from the bottom of the pit. The engineer was even more surprised, when the winding rope began to sway violently in the shaft; clearly, something was wrong – very wrong. A number of

Shaft sinking conditions as they would have been at Douglas Bank Colliery. This was one of the most dangerous occupations in mining. From the Illustrated London News, *28 September 1878.* www.cmhrc.co.uk

Douglas Bank Colliery c.1930. Peter Nadin collection

men on the surface shouted down into the pit, but got no response. Quickly, another party of sinkers was assembled, and a second hoppet was fixed into position, and the men were lowered down the pit. As they neared the bottom, they saw to their sheer horror that the whole of the last section of shaft walling, 13 yards deep and 16 feet in diameter had collapsed. This had all fallen to the bottom of the pit completely burying the other hoppet along with its human cargo.

The signal was given to stop lowering the men, and all was quiet for a while, then the foreman heard voices from under the tangled mess of bricks – someone at least had survived. A working party was sent down, and load after load of rubble, bricks and rock were raised out of the shaft. After some lengthy work, three of the eight men were rescued alive, the rest discovered some time later dead under the bricks and debris. It appeared that the blasting had dislodged half of the shaft walling and, when the first hoppet was being lowered, the rest came down on top of the men, knocking the hoppet on its side. The five dead men were thrown out of the bucket, the other three happily held on and, amazingly, the hoppet provided cover as the rest of the brickwork crashed around them. The dead men were:

Doctor Entwistle, aged 45, married with six children
James Marrow, aged 30, married, but with no children

Lawrence Carney, aged 22, married, with no children
Thomas Doolan, aged 30, married, with one child
William Hardy, aged 23, single.

Eventually, the Douglas Bank Colliery became a productive and profitable pit for the company. In May 1887, work was started on deepening the shafts, which were sunk a further 228 yards (including the sump) from the Cannel Mine down to the Arley Mine. Incredibly, while this work was ongoing, in April 1888, another shaft accident claimed another five lives. The shaft sinkers were being lowered down the pit, when for some reason the hoppet overturned, throwing three men out to their deaths and killing another two who were at the bottom of the pit. The Pemberton Four Feet seam was worked by the pillar and stall method, and by the turn of the century was being worked back towards the shaft, having reached the boundary. Both winding engines at the colliery were made by Messrs Daglish of St Helens in 1865, the one at the North Shaft had two horizontal cylinders 30 inches in diameter, with a 5-feet stroke and Cornish valves. The Douglas Bank Colliery abandoned coal winding on 13 December 1920 when it employed 666 underground men and 186 surface workers. The pit was kept open for a while after this, before being officially abandoned altogether on 17 July 1929, after a credible and profitable working life of sixty-five years. The colliery site was not cleared until 1950 by the NCB.

(14) California Pit, Kirkless Hall Colliery, Wigan: 12 September 1865

... the cage was submerged in the dank depths of the dark water, and there was no sign of life.

The Kirkless Hall Coal and Iron Company worked a number of mines, coke and ironworks around and across the Leeds and Liverpool Canal from the Kirkless Hall Farm, Wigan. These extensive works would have been bounded today by Green Lane, Falkirk Drive and Gale Lane. The California Pit had been in existence for a long time, and had an output as great as any of the other pits in the Wigan district, even though only one seam, the Arley Mine was worked. At the time of this accident the pit employed between 300 and 400 colliers and drawers. However, the previous Saturday was 'Pay Saturday', consequently the following Monday was 'Play Monday' when most of the colliers, having money to spend, would have been worse for drink. It appears that the headaches, or the money, lasted to the following day, Tuesday 12 September 1865, when just 277 lamps were handed out to the men, who descended the pit at the usual time that morning.

With the day's work done, the colliers began ascending the pit shaft, and by a quarter to four that afternoon, about one hundred men had been raised up the 315 yards deep pit. Below ground the men and boys gathered to await their turn to be raised up the pit – eight more colliers and boys were placed in the upper of the two decked cage by the hooker on, and the signal was given to the engineman to raise them up the shaft. The cage rose slowly from the depths of the mine, and the sounds of the waiting colliers far below faded away. The cage slowed down when nearing the pit bank at about 45 yards below the surface. The engineman suddenly noticed the winding rope slip off the conical winding drum, and the subsequent jerk snapped the steel rope, the cage then plunging into the depths of the pit, taking its freight of men and boys with it. Those at the bottom realised what was happening and rushed back, just in time to see the cage crash through the thick balks of timber covering the water sump at the bottom of the shaft. Panic ensued as the men below rushed forward to help, if help was of use, to those in the cage. It was soon realised that they were beyond any aid since the cage was submerged in the dank depths of the dark water, and there was no sign of life. At the surface, a temporary capstan was quickly brought into use and, by five o'clock that day, five men were lowered down the shaft. There was little damage to the shaft itself, the cage was fixed by means of steel guide rods in the shaft, although the last 100 yards or so of these steel rods had followed the cage into the sump, and piled up on top of it. As it was deemed that there was no hope at all of the men and boys having survived the drop, those men still below were raised to the surface, before the recovery of the dead commenced. By twenty-past six, all these waiting men, totalling about one hundred, had been hauled to the top of the mine.

Preparations were then begun to recover the unfortunate victims. The cage was fastened to a strong capstan rope, and raised, creaking and groaning out of the

Drawing the coal from the working face or stall was a job for the younger underground worker, who then progressed to actually getting the coal. This illustration shows the work undertaken by the drawers which would have been typical of the California Pit. From the Illustrated London News, *28 September 1878.* www.cmhrc.co.uk

sump hole. The water spewed forth and empted the death trap. The cage was of course completely wrecked, and those inside were fearfully crushed and mangled. As required and instructed, the men were carefully removed from the crumpled structure, and raised to the surface. Here they were placed on carts to be taken to the *Running Horses Inn* at Aspull, to await the coroner's inquest. All eight were named as:

> James Ramsdale, aged 23, of Hindley, a collier, single
> John Dunn, aged 17, of Hindley, a drawer, single
> George Ingham, aged 17, of Hindley, a drawer, single
> John Holland, aged 20, of Ince, a collier, single
> William Bradshaw, aged 18, of Hindley, single
> Robert Fletcher, aged just 12 years, of New Springs, a pony driver
> Robert Eatock, aged 46, of Hindley, collier, married with six children
> Edward Anderton, aged 27, a collier, married with two children

It was never determined how, or indeed why the rope should have slipped off the winding drum, causing this mining disaster. The rope was of steel, and about 3¾ inches in diameter, and had only been on the drum since 13 May that year. It was calculated to be able to have taken the strain of ten or twelve tons, more than of sufficient strength for normal winding operations. When the California Pit of the Kirkless Hall Colliery was abandoned in 1898, the events of 20 August 1867, would have been a distant memory for most, save those who lost their loved ones that day. There was an even greater tragedy at the Kirkless Hall Colliery earlier, in June 1847, when thirteen men and boys were killed through an explosion, thought to have been caused through a shot being fired, which ignited the coal, and caused the disaster.

(15) Mesne Lea Colliery, Worsley, Manchester: 30 May 1867

... it was considered to be a safe pit and, as a consequence, candles were used by the men rather than Davy lamps.

The Mesne Lea Colliery was an old pit dating from 1824, and was located off Walkden Road near its junction with the East Lancashire Road, opposite Mesne Lea Lane. Mr Peter Nightingale worked the pit at the time of this explosion, and the shaft was 181 yards deep. From the bottom of the shaft a tunnel ran 128 yards, to the start of a down brow, or sloping tunnel, which was 280 yards long. Further levels were driven off this down brow at right angles running eastwards for nearly 800 yards. It was on these levels that the coal was being worked at the time of the accident, the seam being the Wigan Seven Feet. Very little gas (methane) was ever found at the Mesne Lea Colliery, it was considered to be a safe pit and, as a consequence, candles were used by the men rather than Davy lamps.

It was, however, normal at all collieries at this time, for the fireman to examine all the underground workings with a safety lamp before the men were allowed to go to their work places. But on this day, this duty may not been done; this was, however, speculation since the fireman himself was one of the victims of the disaster, and no other evidence was forthcoming. At six o'clock on the morning of 30 May 1867, ten colliers went down the pit to start their day's work. Half and

All that the women and children could do was sit and wait for news of their loved ones whilst frantic attempts continued to get the living (and the dead) out of the mine. This might have been the scene at Mesne Lea Colliery, Worsley, in 1867. From the Illustrated London News. www.cmhrc.co.uk

hour later, one of the men came up the pit and informed the manager, Mr R Halliday, that there had been a fire followed by an explosion in the Seven Feet Seam. There was no indication of explosion on the surface, indeed everything appeared to be working normally, and Halliday was in some doubt as to the statement's accuracy. However, he got some assistance, and descended the pit, where he discovered that there had indeed been an ignition of gas. Unlike most other pit explosions there was no loud report, or any considerable damage done, save some harm to a number of displaced bricks at some stopping, used to control the flow of air. There was though a good deal of afterdamp, and concern was being felt for those at the far end of the workings. Efforts were made to restore the ventilation by rebuilding the stoppings, and progress was slowly made into the further reaches of the mine.

Between nine and ten o'clock, two colliers were found: James Seddon and Thomas Brundrett. They were alive, but only just, both dreadfully burnt. In fact the injuries to Seddon proved too much, and he died before the rescue parties could raise him up the pit. Brundrett faired no better. He was raised to the pit bank but died within minutes. A further search revealed the dead bodies of five others, including that of the fireman, Enoch Yates, and all were disfigured. The last body was removed from the pit at half-past seven o'clock, and when it had been ascertained that life was extinct, the dead were removed to their respective homes to await an inquest into the explosion. Credit must be given to Mr Halliday, the pit manager; he toiled relentlessly in searching for the men for well over five hours, and in appalling conditions. When he was raised from the pit he was so overcome by fatigue and the foul air that he collapsed into a state of insensibility. Peter Nightingale (the owner of the pit), Mr J Higson (son of the Mines Inspector), Mr Ridyard (surveyor for the Bridgwater estates), and Mr Wallwork (agent to the Bridgwater Trustees), also played an important part in the rescue; they too were much fatigued. At length they were able to give an account of those who perished at the Mesne Lea Colliery that day. The death toll was not large in terms of colliery explosions, but it brought stark realisation to the every day risks taken in mining coal. The dead were listed as:

John Seddon, of Little Hulton, aged 60 years, left a family
James Seddon, of Little Hulton, aged 25, son of the above
Thomas Brundrett of Worsley, aged 26, single
John Johnson, of Worsley, aged about 40, left four children
James Johnson, of Worsley aged 25, nephew of the above, single
Enoch Yates, Little Hulton, aged 37, left a wife and seven children
Thomas Houghton, Little Hulton, aged 45 and single

The cause of the disaster was attributed to the gas being ignited at one of the open flames used by the men. By 1896, the colliery was being worked by the Worsley Mesnes Colliery Co., of Wigan. John Corner was the manager at that time, and George Morris the under-manager. The pit employed 205 men and boys below ground and thirty-two surface workers. By the end of the First World War the number employed at the pit had risen to over 800. Mesne Lea Colliery was finally abandoned in January 1924, although there is some evidence that one of the shafts was retained as a pumping station for other pits in the locality since it is marked on a 1930s map as 'Pumping station'.

(16) Little Delf Mine, Garswood Colliery: 20 August 1867

Some of the deceased were dreadfully burnt and disfigured, and could only be recognised by their clothing.

The Garswood Colliery was located at Stanley Bank, south of the Old Garswood Park, which is north west of Blackbrook, between St Helens and Haydock. The pit was not new to coal mining disasters, since just the year before, on 13 May 1866, thirteen men and boys perished in an explosion; but the events of 20 August 1867 proved to be greater in loss. The Garswood Colliery at this time consisted of four mines, or four seams (Main Delf, Little Delf, Rushy Park and Four Feet Mines), each worked from a separate shaft. At some time the pit was connected underground with the nearby Laffak Colliery, the men from the latter pit descending to the Laffak workings by way of the Garswood shafts. Indeed, the Laffak and Garswood Colliery Company worked the pit in 1869. A branch of the St Helens Canal served the collieries, as did a loop of the London Midlands and Southern Railway Co. The accident occurred at the Little Delf Mine, which was being worked at a depth of 460 yards, and 1,000 yards from the pit bottom. Here, was what was known as the 'top level' that ran in the direction of the Old Garswood Park. This tunnel inclined upwards, to a remote part of the workings, so consequently there was always a danger of gas (being lighter than air) collecting there. Just fourteen men and boys were working in this district.

At ten minutes to twelve on Tuesday 20 August 1867, an explosion occurred in that part of the mine, and all those working there were killed. It was not a loud explosion as many men in other parts of the workings were unaware of what had happened. However, once it was known, all the men and boys were withdrawn from the pit and it now remained to find those who were not so fortunate. A party of volunteers was quickly formed, consisting of Thomas Molyneux, senior, manager of the pit, his son of the same name, the under-manager, William Tickle who was in charge of the surface of the mine, and a number of colliers. All these were employed at the Garswood Colliery, and although other volunteers from neighbouring collieries were soon on the scene, their help was not needed. Within a few hours, the rescuers succeeded in reaching the unfortunates, and on being found they were removed to the shaft. In consequence of the large number of relatives and mourners at the pit bank, it was decided not to raise those who had died until night time. Those involved in the fatal accident that day at the Garswood Colliery were named as:

Joseph Topping, fireman, of Haydock
Thomas Anders, a collier, of Park Road, Parr
William Cheetham junior, a collier, of Park Road, Parr
William Chestworth, a collier, of Haydock
John Eden, son of Mrs Mathers, whose husband was murdered near St Helens, a few weeks previously
Anthony Fillingham, a collier, of Finger Post, Parr
Henry Winstanley, collier, of Haresfinch
William Brown, collier, of John Hill Brow, Parr
William Baron, driver, of John Hill Brow, Parr
John Leadbetter, driver, of Highlands Brow, Parr
Henry Wright, pony driver, of Copper House Row, Ashton
Thomas Radcliffe, of Gerard's Bridge, St Helens
Thomas Wilkinson, jigger, of Coal Pit Lane, Parr

Although the above list only names thirteen dead, it is known that fourteen perished that day. Some of the deceased were dreadfully burnt and disfigured, and could only be recognised by their clothing. On being raised, the dead were

News spread rapidly following any disaster and crowds gathered quickly; such would be the scene at Garswood Colliery in 1867. From the Illustrated London News. www.cmhrc.co.uk

conveyed to the *Owl's Nest* public house near the pit to await the coroner's inquest. The cause of the accident was never determined, but it was conjectured that the fireman, Joseph Topping, was firing a charge of powder, and the shot blew out, igniting the gas. Strange to say, the explosion of May 1866, barely fourteen months before, was also caused by Topping firing a charge, when thirteen lives were lost. He escaped with his life on that occasion, but not this time. The Garswood Colliery continued until it was finally abandoned in 1875. It should not be confused with the Garswood Hall Colliery, now the site of the Three Sisters Country Park, which was abandoned in 1958.

(17) Springs Pit, Hindley Green Colliery, Hindley: 26 November 1868

... some of the boys killed had clean and healthy looking faces, and looked as if they were in slumber ...

As time progressed in coal mining history the collieries got larger and deeper and, as a consequence, employed more and more men and boys. When explosions did occurred at pits such as these, the effects were disastrous in terms of lives lost. Such was the explosion at the Springs Pit of the Hindley Green Colliery on

26 November 1868, at Hindley Green, to the east of Wigan. Today, the site of the former colliery is bounded by Coal Pit Lane, Close Lane, Leigh Road and the Atherton Road. Even in 1868 the pits were stated to have been the oldest mines in the district. A previous explosion is recorded at the Hindley Green Colliery back in August 1848, when five persons were killed, including three thirteen-year-old lads. However, the section of the pits where this explosion took place had only been working some four or five years. The pit was formerly worked by John Scowcroft, a name retained, and which later became a limited liability company, working under the title of Messrs John Scowcroft and Company.

The colliery was a major employer at Hindley Green, nearly 300 men and boys working there. The downcast shaft at the pit was 300 yards deep, and 12 feet in diameter. The pit was ventilated at the upcast shaft, which was 10 feet in diameter, by means of a furnace, and all the men worked with locked safety lamps. All in all, it appeared to have been a well-run mine. The seam worked was the Arley Mine, which was about 4 feet 6 inches thick, and said 'not to have given out any extra-ordinary amounts of gas.' Levels were driven out from the bottom of the downcast shaft in three or four directions to work the coal. At six o'clock the fireman made his preliminary inspection of the pit, and his report stated that the pit was in a perfectly satisfactory condition. The men descended soon after and proceeded to their place of work. At twenty minutes before nine o'clock, an explosion took place in the workings but it was not a violent one, in fact some of the men on hearing a thud, thought that there had simply been a roof fall in the western workings. The ventilation current did reverse, but returned to its correct course within a few minutes. There was no damage to either shafts. The underlooker, a man named Ellis, knew however that something was amiss. He was at the upcast shaft near the furnace. Ellis signalled to be raised to the surface and the manager, Thomas Southworth, was informed of the circumstances. Southworth ordered water to be pumped into the downcast shaft to increase the ventilation underground. Mean-while, a steady and growing number of volunteers lined up to begin the rescue operations, and soon crowds of relatives, wives, mothers and children began to gather around the pit bank, to await news of those still below.

As the rescue teams were being organised, the cages were lowered and, incredibly, men and boys were raised alive, although some were concussed and suffering from the effects of the afterdamp – but at least some of those below were to survive. Groups of miners from other local pits came to give what assistance they could, and at length it was time to explore the workings for survivors, or the dead. The first of those to be found were near the upcast shaft, terribly burnt, not by the explosion, but by the flames from the ventilation boiler being sucked back when the air reversed.

The movement of the explorers was both arduous and slow, respiration was difficult due to the afterdamp, and the delay was adding to the concern of those walled-in by the deadly gas. Another man was found, apparently dead, but brought back to life by artificial respiration, and quickly removed from the pit. At last, the extremity of the workings was penetrated and, six hours after the explosion, the Hindley Green Colliery gave up the last of its victims. It was a terrible toll, sixty-two men and boys having perished.

The condition of the deceased varied. Some of the boys who were killed had clean and healthy looking faces, and looked as if they were simply in slumber – they had perished through suffocation through the afterdamp. Others were much burnt, the flesh torn from the bone, hanging and scorched. Among the corpses in the workshops on the surface lay two brothers named Tyldesley. They were two of the four sons of a woman who had only recently lost her husband. Her other two sons were also in the pit at the time, one escaping, and the other caught by the blast and, suffering no great injury, brought out alive. Among those killed were a number of young lads, drawers in the pit, and youths barely in their teens. Others were married and left large families to mourn their loss. Joseph Highton, for example, left a widow and ten children, one of which, Richard, aged just twelve years, died in the disaster; whilst Isaac Sergeant left a widow and nine children.

One can only imagine the grief at Hindley Green Village and the surrounding area in the days that followed, the coffins, and the endless funerals, all the mourning. The village was thrown into the national headlines, but only for a few days, and then forgotten – left to grieve that terrible day on its own.

Forty-five (of sixty-two) names of those 'confirmed dead' are found in the early newspaper reports. Identification of all fatalities from contemporary reports was complex because of some men were so badly burned that they were not expected to live, others were 'still missing' and so on:

Ashurst, Thomas, single
Blackburn, Peter, aged 15, West Leigh
Bromilow, Thomas, single
Connor, Thomas, 15, Hindley
Crook, Joseph, 53, Ince
Dearden, William, single
Evans, Thomas
Greenhalgh, Thomas, married with two children
Gregory, William, 14, Hindley
Grundy, Abraham, single
Grundy, William, single
Halliwell, William, 16, whose father was also killed
Haslam, William, married with two children
Hayes, Alfred, youth
Highton, Richard, 12, son of Joseph Higton
Holcroft, Thomas, married
Houghton, James, married
Johnson, William, married
Kaye, Thomas, married, one child
Kirkpatrick, William, boy
Latham, James, 26, West Leigh
Longton, Thomas, single
Markland, William, married
Marsh, Jo, boy
Mellor, William, 15, Swan Lane
Morris, James, youth
Parrington, Samuel, single

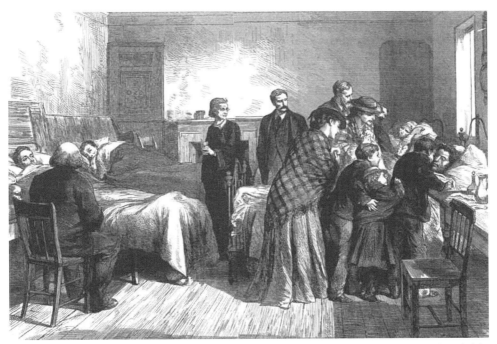

Any men and boys that did survive a mining disaster would be taken to their homes and tended by family and friends. This scene may have occurred at Springs Pit, Hindley Green. From the Illustrated London News, *15 February 1890.* www.cmhrc.co.uk

Pilkington, married, one child
Pilling, William, boy
Prescot, Thomas, 14, West Leigh
Ramsdale, Thomas, boy
Rhodes, Benjamin, single
Rostern (?), Thomas, 15, Hindley
Sergeant, Isaac
Shannon, Peter, 30, Leigh, married with five children
Smethhurst, Isaac, Sharples
Smith, Daniel, boy of about 12
Southern, George, boy
Southern, James, boy
Starkey, John
Tyldesley, Joseph, boy
Tyldesley, William, young man
Woods, James, 17, Hindley
Yates, William, aged 12

The named injured were:

A boy named Ingram of Sandy Lane
John Gerard, Chapel Lane
Hayes (?), married, Colliers Row

Hayes (?), married, Slackyfold
Heyes (?), Married, Colliers Row
Sergeant (?), son of Isaac who was killed
Tyldsley, a boy, Slackfold

We are also informed in the report that 'Three other boys in Hindley Green are also burned severely, but we could not ascertain their names. Three other cases will in all probability terminate fatally. The calamity has deprived twenty women of their husbands, and between fifty and sixty children of their fathers.'

The cause of the explosion could only be guessed at, for those at the seat of the blast had perished, although it was thought that a blown out shot fired by an unskilled person might have been the cause. Today, the site of the former Hindley Green Colliery is taken by works units, playing fields, recreation grounds, and tennis courts. Children now play where their forefathers died all those years ago, deep beneath the ground at their feet. The Hindley Green Colliery was not giving up its minerals easily, for on 15 November 1871, another six miners died at the pit, through a another shotfiring incident that caused a further disaster. The Hindley Green Colliery, and its 'Grammar Pit', the 'Springs Pit', where the above disaster occurred, and 'Arley Yard Pit', were abandoned in 1929, when still worked by J Scowcroft and Co, Ltd. These three pits employed in total 526 men. The 'California Pit' and the 'Engine' Pits', also worked by J Scowcroft were abandoned in 1930, thus bringing to an end the Hindley Green Colliery and its dark and deathly past.

Rescue workers struggle to get the injured and dead to the surface following a pit explosion. Victorian print from the Illustrated London News. www.cmhrc.co.uk

(18) Rainford Colliery: 7 January 1869

. . . the only option now was to seal both pits, and starve the fire of all oxygen.

The Rainford Collieries were located down Sidings Lane off the Ormskirk Road, about a mile from Rainford Village. To the north-east was the Rainford Junction of the London, Midlands and Southern Railway, which had a branch line to the pit. The colliery was in existence from at least 1848 and, in 1854, was being worked by William Harding. It's evident that a number of shafts were sunk in the following years, and by the time of this accident, they were numbered 7 and 8, the downcast shaft being the No. 8 pit, and the upcast the No. 7 pit. At the upcast was a furnace that provided the ventilation for the whole of the workings. The furnace was placed at the entrance to the workings in the Five Feet Seam, which also communicated with the other seam worked at the pit, the Rushy Park Seam.

However, by late 1868, these two seams had been exhausted, although they were not officially abandoned until 1871, when presumably work had started in a new seam being sunk to, after the Rushy Park and Five Feet Seams had been worked out. This shaft sinking was ongoing at the time of the accident in January 1869. The underlooker for the whole of the pits worked by the Rainford Colliery Company was Enoch Cheetham. On Thursday afternoon of 7 January 1869, he was informed that the coal near the ventilation furnace at the upcast shaft was on fire. A number of men were working there, sinking the shafts deeper, and to ventilate the shaft sinkings, a tunnel had been driven connecting both shafts, providing a circuit for the air. Cheetham went down the pit via the downcast pit to investigate what was going on, and ordered all the men out of the connecting tunnel. He then went to the upcast shaft where the fire was reported, and found the coal blazing away at the top of a short down brow, a little distance back from the furnace. He returned to the surface and began to make plans as to how the fire could be extinguished.

It was decided that the best option was to lower water pipes down the downcast shaft, and fight the fire with water. They managed to get eight pipes fitted in the shaft, and calculated that with another four they would be able to reach the fire with the aid of a hose of about 50 feet in length. The underlooker, Enoch Cheetham, left the fireman, James Chadwick, below while he went up the shaft to see to the hose and nozzles. These were sent down the pit, and Cheetham was checking the pipes above ground when he was informed that the pit had 'fired'. This was just a few minutes before midnight on Thursday. Two of those below – Michael Brown and William Glover – signalled to be raised up the pit as they were badly burned from the explosion. A search party was arranged, headed by Cheetham, and the men descended into the burning mine. At the bottom they found two of their comrades, including the fireman, James Chadwick, also badly burnt, and who later died. Passing through a hole in a brick stopping, leading to the upcast shaft, Cheetham began to search for the other three men known to be in that area. The hole had been made so that the fire could be fought, and was about 8 yards from the upcast shaft.

He first came across the dead body of John Smith lying on the ground, and then found Thomas Bullen with his clothes still burning a little further on but he too

Rescue workers in the flooded workings of Rainford Colliery, searching for the living and the dead. From the Illustrated London News. www.cmhrc.co.uk

was dead. With help from a man named Chadwick, both men were got through the hole and to the bottom of the downcast shaft. Returning they found the dead body of Edward Turner, whose clothes were still burning and he too was got through the hole. Cheetham then went back to where the fire was, and found that it was burning fiercely, and extending towards the downcast shaft. The ventilation was strong, much stronger than normal, in spite of clothes put up to slow it down, to prevent it feeding the fire. Cheetham and his searchers returned to the surface, the only option now was to seal both pits, and starve the fire of all oxygen. The upcast shaft was sealed off at the top, and at the downcast shaft, some scaffolding was placed about 4 yards below the surface with the intention of sealing this off at that point.

Having seen to the first of the scaffolding erected, Cheetham, almost at the point of exhaustion, decided to go home and try and get some sleep. The following morning, work was completed on sealing the upcast shaft, and work was begun on completing sealing the downcast shaft. Late Friday night two men, Thomas Whalley and Thomas Barrow, were left to keep an eye on the covers. Early on Saturday, Enoch Cheetham was raised from his bed by a young lad employed at the pit, who informed him that the two men were missing, and it was feared that they had fallen into the shaft. When the shaft was examined, it was found that the scaffold had gone. An attempt was made to get down the pit, but it was impossible, the air was simply un-breathable. The number who died at the Rainford Colliery was eventually put at nine, including the two who fell into the burning pit. The names of those who died in the pit, and in the shaft were:

John Smith, aged 57, a day worker of Rainford, left a widow and two children
Edward Turner, aged 26, a day worker, of Rainford, single
Henry Birchall, aged 49, of Rainford, left a widow and three children
Thomas Bullen, aged 34, sinker, of Rainford
William Glover, aged 40, Rainford
Thomas Whalley, perished in the shaft
Thomas Barrow, perished in the shaft
Michael Brown, 36, sinker, Rainford
James Chadwick, fireman

The explosion at Rainford was thought to have been caused by the action of the fire near the furnace weakening the roof, causing it to fall, releasing a quantity of gas, which then ignited at the fire. The Rainford Colliery was finally abandoned in 1928, when worked by Bromilow and Foster and Co, Ltd. The pit, on abandonment, employed 132 men underground and 59 surface workers. The site of the former colliery is now that of Rainford Nature Reserve. St Helens' Mayor, Councillor Pat Robinson planted a commemorative tree there, when she officially opened a new nature reserve at Siding Lane, Rainford on Wednesday 31 January 2001.

(19) Low Hall Colliery, Platt Bridge: 16 November 1869

Sharratt proceeded slowly in front of his companions and, reaching a side opening, was horrified to find that the place was on fire.

Low Hall Colliery was located off the Bickershaw Road at Platt Bridge, Wigan. The pit finished when the No. 5 pit was abandoned in 1931. The Moss Hall Coal Company operated the Colliery, where eight shafts were worked altogether. There was a remarkable incident at the Low Hall Colliery which resulted in the death of Loudovic Berry, an engine driver at the pit. Mr Berry was driving *Dorothy*, his loaded train of thirteen wagons when the ground under the track opened up over the old New Zealand pit-shaft that had been 'filled in' in 1931. The last wagon fell into the crater taking with it the rest of the train including Mr Berry, plunging down the 12 feet diameter and 334 yards deep shaft. The re-capped shaft can still be seen today, with a small memorial to these sad events. Many people, including his family, feel that Mr Berry's remains should be raised, and also the loco, the latter displayed as a memorial to him and the former miners of the area (see *The Wigan Coalfield* by Alan Davies and Len Hudson, Tempus Publishing).

At the time of the 1869 disaster, it was stated that the pit was a comparatively new one, having been opened out within the last two years. There is a report of an accident at in August 1867, which may indicated when the shaft was being sunk:

John Hart aged about sixteen was killed at the Low Hall Colliery at Hindley near Wigan. His companions William German and William Hart were seriously injured, the accident was in the shaft.

Low Hall Colliery was typical of the many coal mines that worked the South Lancashire Coalfield.
Peter Nadin collection

Three seams that were being worked were the Wigan Five Feet, the Wigan Four Feet, and the Wigan Six Feet, the lowest seam at a depth of 275 yards at the shaft. In the Six Feet Mine, the workings were driven at all points of the compass, but none were further than 550 yards from the shaft bottom. The explosion took place at the No. 5 Pit on the afternoon of Tuesday 16 November. At once a large crowds of onlookers gathered at the pit, as men made frantic efforts to find out how serious the explosion was. By eight o'clock at night eight dead bodies had been removed for the depths of the mine, and twenty-odd searchers were combing the workings for other unfortunates. Owing to the dense afterdamp, the parties proceeded with caution, carrying air with them, going as far as possible, and yet staying within shouting distance of each other. One such party headed by a man named Sharratt, and two others, took one of the main levels. They had travelled about 400 yards when they met some chokedamp, but not sufficient to hold them back. Sharratt proceeded slowly in front of his companions and, reaching a side opening, was horrified to find the place was on fire. He turned around, and all three ran for their lives back to the shaft. The other searchers were informed, and it was decided that all should get out of the pit as quickly as possible. The cage was filled with the men and hastily raised to the pit bank, and the situation below was given to the assembled crowd and management. Soon all the searchers were back on the pit bank safe and well.

John Higson, the Mines Inspector, was at the surface, along with several managers and engineers from neighbouring collieries. They began to assess the situation. Although Sharratt was fully trustworthy, there were some in the crowd who thought he was being needlessly alarmed since there was, after all, no sign of a fire on the surface. A plan of the workings was produced, and Sharratt pointed out where he had seen the fire, and confirmed that it was indeed a large fire. Still, he was doubted by a number of the assembled crowd. Sharratt declared he would say no more, and walked away with tears in his eyes. Eventually, it was decided that no further explorations should take place that night. The following morning several mining engineers and members of management gathered to decide the next course of action. These included Mr Caldwell, one of the owners of the pit, Mr Knowles of Pearson and Knowles, William Bryham of the Rose Bridge Collieries, George Gilroy from Ince Hall Collieries, and the HM Inspector of Mines, John Higson.

At length, after deciding that there had been no change in the appearance of the smoke coming from the No. 5 upcast shaft, they would try and enter the workings.

Accordingly, a party was arranged to descend headed by the underlooker, Green, and several experienced firemen. After half an hour, they returned, and stated that they had been some distance up the north and south roads, and found the going fairly clear. However, it was later found that there was indeed a fire underground, and the number of men and boys still missing numbered eighteen, entombed within the burning mine. It was decided to try and smother the fire by throwing materials into the No. 6 downcast shaft, but this was slow to have any effect. As the pipe work from Rivington Reservoir supplying Liverpool passed close by the colliery, it was decided to seek permission to draw off some of the water, and flood the mine. Peter Higson approved the course of action, and permission was obtained. By the early hours of Thursday morning, 6-inch cast iron pipes had been laid, through which it was calculated would pass 50,000 gallons of water an hour. The water was turned into the upcast shaft at the pit. The effects of the flooding on the mine were soon apparent, the upcast was converted into the downcast and large volumes of smoke rose from the depths. The flooding continued for two days, more than a fortnight later the mine was dewatered, and the bodies finally removed. Twenty-seven men and boys perished at the Low Hall Colliery; the first eight recovered taken to an untenanted farmhouse, about 200 yards from the pit, known as Low Hall Farm, from which the colliery took its name. Those who perished were named as:

William Golding, a boy, Platt Bridge
Richard Hilton, aged 32, Platt Bridge, married with four children
Peter Simm, Platt Bridge, drawer
William Seddon, Ince
James Ormsher, Bickershaw, fireman
James Winstanley, Platt Bridge, jigger
Henry Woods, a boy, Hindley
Robert Walls, aged 15, Platt Bridge, runner in
William Hilton, Platt Bridge, drawer
Samuel Simm, Ince, drawer
John Fairhurst, Platt Bridge, collier
Peter Fairhurst, father of the above, Platt Bridge, collier
Luke (–?–), drawer
Albert Duxbury, collier
Cain Hart, Platt Bridge, drawer
Thomas Pimblett, Platt Bridge, collier
James Slater, Ashton, drawer

George Harrison, Platt Bridge, collier
Peter Dixon, Platt Bridge, collier
William Oliver, Hindley, collier
John Hampson, Platt Bridge, drawer
Peter Bolton, Platt Bridge, collier
Henry Foster, Platt Bridge, drawer
William Hampson, Platt Bridge, day worker
William Ridyard, Platt Bridge, jigger
William Hurst
John Bennett, Spring View, Ince, drawer

By the mid 1890s, the Low Hall Colliery was a major employer at Platt Bridge, the No. 5 Pit with 311 men, the No. 6 had 223 men, and the No. 8 employed 173 men and boys. The colliery was finally abandoned with the closure of the No. 5 Pit in 1931.

(20) Pendleton Colliery, Pendleton: 4 February 1870

The explosion blew out the stemming or clay used to pack the hole, and the flames that followed injured several men, nine of whom died later.

It was John Purcell Fitzgerald who first sank the Pendleton Colliery back in the late 1820s, where mining took place from the Three Foot and Worsley Four Foot seams. The shafts here were originally sunk to a depth of around 650 feet, and almost 27,000 tons of coal was raised at the pit during the first six months of 1832. The *Blackburn Gazette* reported an early accident here on 6 March 1833, stating that

> *a man named Hughes, who had just began work at Mr Fitzgerald's colliery at Pendleton, Manchester, Lancashire fell down the shaft 64 yards and was killed on the spot.*

This accident must have happened at one of the shaft insets. Two years after the pit was first sunk, it was flooded out, water being a constant problem at the pit. Two new shafts were sunk, each 8 feet in diameter, to reach the drier seams below the Worsley Four Foot seam between 1836 and 1837. Flooding again forced its closure in 1843 and, although it reopened, it was closed down in 1848. In 1852, the colliery was sold to Andrew Knowles and Sons, and under the new owners, the pit was sunk down to the Rams Seam at a depth of 1,545 feet. The workings here dipped away from the shaft and, eventually, the men at Pendleton Colliery were working at a depth of 3,600 feet below ground. This made it the deepest pit in the country, and it remained so for much of its life. In January 1863, water again broke through the shaft lining of the pit, and once again threatened the existence of the mine. The fall of the water down the 1,500 feet deep shaft reversed the ventilation, and the underlookers expressed fears that the ventilation furnace could ignite the coals. Several men went down and put out the fire, and the mine workers along with the sixteen ponies employed there were evacuated. Soon the sumps at the shaft bottom had filled with water, and it was running down the engine brows. It took several days to stem the flow of water and to resume normal working. The upcast shaft was relined in 1872, which reduced the diameter of the pit to just over 7 feet.

Just before the shaft was relined there was an explosion which claimed the lives of six miners. Around ten o'clock on a cold winter's morning of 4 February 1870, Jonathan Chapman was working in the No 2 Level of the Crombouke Seam at the colliery. He had just undercut the coal to a depth of about 2 feet 6 inches at his working place. The normal practice then would have been to cut around both sides of the coal but Chapman chose not to do so. Instead, he simply drilled the coal, set a charge and fired it. The explosion blew out the stemming or clay used to pack the hole, and the flames that followed injured several men, nine of whom later died. The injured men were named as:

William Edward Green, Freehold Terrace, Hankinson Street, Pendleton, aged 18, dangerously burnt.

William Walford, Priory Street, Pendleton, aged 14, dangerously burnt

Roger Hutchinson, Sovereign Street, Pendleton, aged about 28, very severely burnt, delirious, and not likely to recover.

James Radford, Brocade Street, Whit Lane, Pendleton, aged 16, dangerously burnt

Jonathan Chapman, who caused the commotion, of Williamson Street, Charlestown, aged 38, burnt, but not dangerously.

John Williams, Wellington Street, Whit Lane, aged 28, burnt but not dangerously

It is thought that these are the six that later died, all of them taken to the Salford Royal Hospital. The following were injured to a lesser extent, and allowed to be removed to their homes:

John Radford, father of the boy listed above

Joseph Ashton, unmarried

James Thorpe, unmarried

William Lister, unmarried

William Jones, married

James Wolstenholme, married

The inquest on the men and boys who died was held at the *Angel Inn*, Salford. William Halliday said he was in the Albert Mine when the accident happened. He did not hear the report, being about 100 yards away from the where the shot was fired, but felt the wind from the blast. He knew something was wrong, so went towards the engine brow but, smelling the powder, he decided to go another way round. First, he came across Joseph Ashton, a boy, who was badly burnt. Others soon came to help, and they next found another lad named William Walford, who was also badly burnt. They then came across the shotfirer, Chapman, who was sent up the pit along with young Walford. Continuing the search, they came across John Redford, who was near the engine brow, and James Redford his son, who was lying a few yards away on the other side of the brow. They next saw John Williams, James Thorpe; Hutchinson, Green and Wolstenholme had already been taken out of the pit. It appeared to the rescuers on examining the hole where the shot was fired that the stemming had blown out. The coal had not been cut at the sides. Other witnesses were called, many giving the same evidence. The coroner addressed the jury, remarking that, according to the evidence of the witnesses, there was no firedamp or gas in the mine. He thought that the jury

Crowds soon begin to gather at the pit-head, Pendleton Colliery, following news of the explosion. From the Illustrated London News, *20 October 1877.* www.cmhrc.co.uk

could come to no other conclusion than that the deceased miners had been burnt by the powder flame. The question of whether they would recommend anything for the future, as to the distance which the men should be away from shotfiring would be up to them. The jury returned their verdict as follows:

> *That the deceased came to their deaths accidentally from the effects of powder flame, in consequence of the shot being blown out. Secondly, that the flame was not accelerated by inflammable gas, and thirdly, that in all cases of firing shots, the workmen should be at a distance of 50 yards from the shot hole.*

In 1891, two new shafts were started at the Pendleton Colliery, each 16 feet in diameter. However, at a depth of around 120 feet, the sinkers broke into some old uncharted workings. These flooded the new shafts and caused a great deal of subsidence on the surface so that the new shafts had to be abandoned. Another five lives were lost at the pit in November 1925 through the floor upheaving. The Pendleton Colliery, which was located off Whit Lane at Pendleton on the south western side, was finally abandoned in April 1939. At the time Pendleton Colliery was being worked by Manchester Collieries Ltd, and employed 291 underground men and 140 surface workers. The closure was brought about through the exhaustion of economic workings in the remaining Rams Seam. Close by the pit was the Manchester, Bolton and Bury Canal by which much of Pendleton Colliery output was sent. Today, all that remains nearby is Collier

Street, which reminds us of Pendleton's coal mining past. All other traces of the pit have been removed, along with that section of the Manchester, Bolton and Bury Canal.

(21) Bryn Hall Colliery, Bryn: 19 August 1870

Mutilated bodies of both men and horses were found lying a short distance from the pit bottom.

The Bryn Hall Colliery dated from around 1856, when owned by Smith & Sons, and on 20 January 1866, the *Colliery Guardian* informed its readers that the Bryn Hall Colliery and works at Ashton near Wigan were for sale. It appears to have been purchased by W & J B Crippin, who are listed as the owners of the pit in a mines list for the year 1869 and they were still the owners when the pit blew up the following year. The Bryn Hall Colliery was located off Bryn Gates Lane, to the north east of what is today the Three Sisters Recreation Area near Ashton-in-Makerfield. Besides the extensive siding along the LMS Railway, another tramway ran up to the Leeds and Liverpool Canal near Ince Moss. Under W & J B Crippin, the pit worked the Four Feet Seam, but soon they began to open out the Wigan Nine Feet Seam. The first intimation that anything was amiss on the

A plan of the workings at Bryn Hall Colliery following the explosion, taken from the reports of the mines inspector. Author's collection

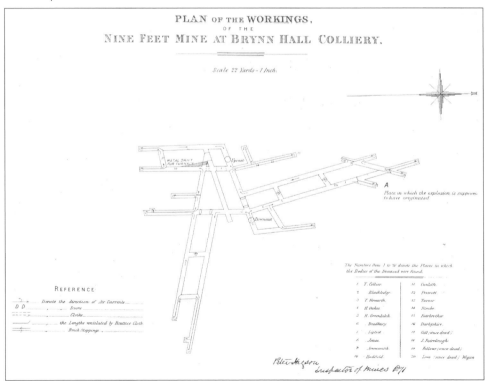

79

morning of Friday 19 August 1870 was on the surface of the pit. At half-past nine the surface workers, along with residents from miles around were startled by a loud report from the upcast shaft, followed by a fearful belching of vivid scarlet flames and smoke. There was no doubting in the mining community of what had happened, their worst fears had been realised, the pit had fired. No coals were raised at the upcast shaft, the mouth of which was covered by a 'jiddy' or move-able platform, often used in sinking operations, to protect the men below from falling objects. The jiddy, made of strong steel, was literally scattered in bits over a large area, including the nearby railway, and for a time the shaft could not be approached by anyone. At the downcast shaft the cage was broken and crashed into the depths of the pit shaft, taking with it the guides and pumping pipes, and anything else in its wake. Soon the scene of the calamity was flocked to by large crowds eager to gather news of those still below.

Arriving, too, were the proprietors of other local collieries, keen to give advice and help where they could. These included Mr William Smithurst of Bryn Collieries, Messrs Mercer and Evans of the Park Lane Pits; and Mr Latham and Mr Wright of the Low Hall Pits. William Pickard, the miners' agent, was also in the scene within the hour. The first business was to bring to the pit-bank the workmen employed in the Four Feet Seam, which was not affected by the explosion – these numbered around a hundred in total. This involved setting up a hoppet, a large bucket in the shaft, and raising the men by that means. The searching parties were then free to start their grim task of exploring the workings of the Nine Feet Seam but they were met by fearful confusion. The doors between the two pit shafts regulating the air were blown down and shattered to pieces, and air stoppings, also put up to control the air current, had been blasted away. Mutilated bodies of both men and ponies were found lying a short distance from the pit bottom.

Amazingly, fifteen men were found alive, although suffering from the after-damp, and were quickly placed in the hoppet and raised to the pit bank. More dead bodies were found in a level that ran north and south and, in another level that ran east, there were strong indications of afterdamp. Here, too, were large volumes of smoke, and it became known that the coal was on fire. It became necessary for the searchers to retreat to the shaft, and be raised up, so as to decide their next option. Those waiting above had become increasingly alarmed for those below and at the great mass of smoke coming out of the upcast shaft. It was, as one individual put it 'smoking like a factory chimney', a clear indication that there was indeed a fire below.

For a number of hours it was considered that any attempts at rescue should be delayed and then, suddenly, the smoke at the shaft stopped. The fire, it appeared, had extinguished itself. Further exploration revealed that the source of the fire was some brattice cloth, which had caught alight during the initial explosion, being coated with tar it gave off large amounts of smoke, but soon burnt itself out. As darkness approached, another party of explorers descended the mine headed by Mr Watkin, manager of the Pemberton Collieries. They soon came across another five dead men, and one so badly injured that he, too, died within a few minutes of being raised. Soon, all the dead had been raised to the surface of the pit, the number totalling twenty, with many others injured and burnt. The first list of the victims, only names eighteen, and it must be presumed that two of the injured later died from their wounds. The dead victims were named as:

Thomas Collier, aged 17, of Ashton, a drawer, single
James Blackledge, aged 13, of Ince, a drawer
Thomas Howarth, aged 20 of Pemberton, a drawer
Robert Greenhalgh, aged 21, of Ince, a drawer
Samuel Bradburn, aged 15, of Ashton, pony driver
John Lowe, aged 43, of Bridge Street, Wigan, a fireman
Joseph Gill, aged 34, Ince Bar, collier, left a wife and three children
William Jones, aged 29, Low Green, collier, left a wife
John Liptrot, aged 29, Hindley, collier
Edward Arrowsmith, aged 23, Wigan, drawer
James Hadfield, aged 35, Goose Green, collier, left a wife and two children
James Cunliffe, aged 35, Downall Green, drawer, single
James Prescott, aged 31, Goose Green, drawer, left a wife and two children
Samuel Turner, aged 43, Wigan, collier, left a wife
John Bymbo, Downall Green, collier
Thomas Darbyshire, Downall Green, collier
James Fairclough, 22, Heath Lane, Ashton, left a wife and one child
Henry Oakes, Downall Green, collier

There was another explosion at the Bryn Hall Colliery, on 6 June 1873, happily with not the great loss of life as the above, but nevertheless six persons were killed, and much damage was done to the pit. The mineral lease at the Bryn Hall Colliery

All eyes turn to the pit at Bryn Ball Colliery and watch in horror the flames spewing from the mouth of the shaft, their worst fears becoming reality. Typical scene from the Illustrated London News, *5 May 1851.* www.cmhrc.co.uk

Bryn Hall Colliery. Author's collection

was granted from under Mr Gerald's Estate. The Bryn Hall Colliery, Nos. 2 & 3 were abandoned in November 1945, when the pits employed 522 men, and were worked by the Bryn Hall Colliery Company Limited. The name of the pit is spelt Brynn, with a double 'n' in a number of publications.

Part Three
Immense loss of lives
1871–1910

(22) Moss Colliery, Ince: 6 September 1871

On arrival [at the pit bottom] *the men in the hoppet were met by a group of colliers dreadfully injured and crying out for water and medical attention, some of them beyond help.*

Ince-in-Makerfield was the place near where the Moss Colliery disaster of 1871 occurred, standing astride the A577, about a mile from Wigan. The pit was a relatively new one having only been opened a few years previously, and was worked by Messrs Pearson and Knowles. The shafts here were sunk to a depth of some 580 yards where they intercepted the Cannel Seam. Work was still going on in the upcast shaft by way of further sinking to reach the Arley Seam lower down. Although most of the mining took place in the Cannel Mine, some twelve months previous development was in the Wigan Nine Feet. This seam lay at 480 yards down the shafts, and the workings at the time of the disaster only extended some 270 yards. Near the mouthing of the Four Foot Seam, a short distance above the Wigan Nine Foot Seam, was placed a ventilation furnace, this being the upcast shaft and the place where further sinking was going on some 100 yards below.

Moss was considered to be adequately ventilated, indeed one of the under-lookers, named Prescott, stated that when he left the Nine Feet to go up to the ventilation furnace just five minutes before it fired that *A man might have gone through with a lighted torch with out danger.* The day of the disaster was Wednesday 6 September 1871. Down the pit were sixty-eight men and boys, at work in the Nine Foot Seam and nearly the same number in the Cannel Mine. In addition, there were six shaft sinkers at work in the upcast shaft. Just before eleven o'clock, three miners stepped into the cage at the upcast shaft to descend the mine. They were about halfway down when the mine exploded. From the upcast shaft, a thick plume of dense smoke rose into the air.

News of the explosion soon spread and, at the pit-top, shawled women with anxious faces waited for news of their loved ones, the children staring wide-eyed, and clutching their mothers clothes, all waiting for news. The government Inspector of Mines was in Wigan at the time, and he too was soon at the scene. So too was Mr Pickard the miners' agent, who lived at Ince and was one of the first to arrive. The shafts were inspected and found to be badly damaged, the cage at the downcast shaft having been thrown from its position. Nearby a cloth cap was found which, it was presumed, belonged to one of the miners who were descending the pit when the explosion occurred. As can be imagined, great anxiety was now being expressed for those below. After one and a half hours, a repair was made to the winding engine at the downcast shaft, and a hoppet (a large bucket) was placed on the end of the rope. This was lowered into the mine, then several minutes later it was raised again – empty. Again, the hoppet was lowered in the hope that anyone still living might be able to ascend; again it came up empty.

As is common in these cases, there is never any lack of volunteers, three men were soon lowered down in the hoppet, cautiously as far as the Cannel Mine. They returned, to the joy of the crowds, with five colliers who announced that all the men in that seam were safe. The hoppet was lowered and raised in quick succession in order to get these men out before the oncome of the afterdamp and, within a few hours, all were out. An exploration party consisting of Mr J Bryham, Mr Pickard (the miners' agent), Mr Carter the underground manager, and Mr W Hampson descended the upcast shaft. They stopped first at the Four Foot Seam, where the ventilation furnace was placed to check on the condition of the workings there. No-one it was surmised was working there, yet at the mouthing there were three men: Henry Prescott the underlooker; also the furnace man and a brick-setter, all three alive. They were quickly conveyed up the shaft, and a further attempt was made for the descent to the Nine Foot Seam. On arrival, the men in the hoppet were met by a group of colliers dreadfully injured and crying out for water and medical attention, some beyond help.

The scene presented one of total dereliction and destruction, timbers and roof supports were scattered about, coal tubs were bent and broken, and the air was thick with a sulphurous smog. As many of the men that could be found alive were quickly sent up the shaft where, at the top, tea and other refreshment were sent back down to the sufferers on the return journey. Mr Pickard was exploring the further workings, and ascended up the shaft about two o'clock. He reported that the sides of the pit were on fire, and preparations for a number of hand-held extinguishers were sent for. A party led by J Bryham descended again into the pit in an attempt to quell the underground fires. Around twenty-past three, the column of smoke from the upcast shaft ceased for a few seconds, followed by a low booming noise. Another explosion had occurred, not as big as the first, but still causing great concern for the safety of the exploring parties still below ground. The hoppet was swiftly raised and out stepped Mr Bryham and a number of rescuers. The others quickly followed. None were injured, although some men had been thrown about by the draught from the explosion, which took place in other workings.

A consultation followed between the officials, who concluded that further explorations would be useless, since there could now be little doubt as to the fate of the men still in the mine. To add further risk to the men attempting a rescue, it was decided to seal the pits and block off the air to the fires underground. Twenty-five colliers, thirty-three drawers, six shaft sinkers, one fireman, two hookers-on, one winder-up (also one of the men brought out of the Nine Feet workings had since died from his injuries), and the banksman. Seventy perished all told, and the wrath of the Moss Colliery Disaster was not finished, as we shall see.

The road to Moss Colliery, and the pit bank itself was covered in a mass of bereaved and distressed relatives and friends, with a great feeling of utter despair that only mining communities can share. Women whose husbands worked in the neighbouring collieries came to give their support for they knew in their hearts that colliery explosions have no friends. Tomorrow it may be have been them who are mourning. By Thursday night, both shafts at the colliery were covered over with brickwork, and puddled with clay to deprive the underground fires of oxygen.

It was not until Wednesday 20 September, two weeks after the initial explosion, that the decision was taken to remove the seals on top of the shafts. The puddling clay was slowly removed, first from the upcast shaft, and then followed by about a half the planking. Vast amounts of highly explosive gases immediately issued forth, so combustible that they 'fired' the Davy lamps up to a distance of 10 yards from the shaft. After a while, these gases weakened, and work began on the downcast shaft. With the removal of the clay, the first board was taken up and an immense 'suck' was observed, an indication that the ventilation was taking its proper course. All seemed well, and it appeared that an exploration party could be arranged to descend the pit within a few hours. About three o'clock Jacob Higson was looking over the rim of the upcast shaft, and remarked to Thomas Knowles one of the colliery proprietors '*That all seemed quiet below, and that within a few hours they should be able to descend.*' He had scarcely finished the sentence, when he heard a great rush of wind from below, followed by a long blast of fire.

The men and officials around the top of the upcast shaft were blown tens of yards on to the nearby railway. Those that could, looked up in shock and horror and they saw a dark and dense thick cloud of smoke rise from the other shaft; and a split second later vivid red flames filled the shaft and shot 30 yards and more above the headgear. At this shaft, nearly everyone in the vicinity was severely injured, and at least two of them killed outright. John Knowles, son of one of the owners of the pit, had a broken leg and other injuries. Mr Pickard, the miners' agent was so badly injured that he had to be helped to his home as he could hardly walk. The foreman joiner, Farrimond, and a man named Peak were injured so severely that they died the same day. Two bodies were recovered from the scaffolding just below the rim of the downcast shaft, and were identified as men named Ashurst and Walsh. They were described as being terribly mangled, having taken the full force of the blast. The reports of the day go into horrific details, and tell us that '*Some time after the explosion, a limb was found a considerable distance from the shaft which was thought to have belonged to Ashurst.*'

A good while after, it was realised that another man, named Shuttleworth, was missing. He too was working on the scaffolding, and it was assumed he was caught by the force of the blast and precipitated to the bottom of the shaft. The force of the explosion showed in the head gearing, built from large balks of timbers, which were smashed like matchwood. The hoppet that had been hanging over the shaft, was thrown up and tangled with the remains of the headgear. So loud was the report of the blast that it was heard several miles away, and the flames were seen by many in the borough. Messengers, sent out for doctors to attend to the injured, were stopped by people standing at their doorways, who begged for information, fearing that another pit in the neighbourhood had fired. Again crowds assembled on the Moss pit bank, whose numbers swelled and had to be controlled by police and mine officials in case of another blast. The only option open to them now appeared to be that of flooding the mine. The work went on into the early hours, the men knocking off about three o'clock. Three constables were left on duty overnight, and shortly before four o'clock noticed that the smoke from the shafts was increasing in quantity, and approached for a better vantage point. They got within 30 yards when immense sheet of flames shot from the bowels of the mine high into the air, followed by a loud blast. The policemen ran for their lives through the fields as debris showered down on them from all directions. The shaking of the ground was felt in villages four and 5 miles away. A repetition took place around six o'clock, which, while not on the same scale, set

Thousands of gallons of water were poured into Moss Pit to try and quell the fire below ground. This is a typical scene, taken from The Graphic, *21 September 1878.* www.cmhrc.co.uk

fire to the headgear and the winding house. The Borough fire engine was called in, but its hoses were far too short to reach and at half-past eight the headgear collapsed, the huge cast iron wheels breaking and landing on top of the shaft, but failed to fall down it. A number of minor outbursts continued through out the day, though none were as large as the one in the early morning. Work continued in flooding the pit, the loud reports from down below diminished to 'growls' until these, too, whimpered out; Moss pit was not giving up its victims easily. Soon there were five pumps filling the mine with an estimated 50,000 gallons of water per hour. Over the next few weeks, this process continued until all the mine workings were filled with water.

Coroner's inquests were called week after week at the *Railway Tavern* at Ince, where the colliery proprietors gave a progress report on how the bodies where going to be recovered. This was no easy job as firstly the pit had to be de-watered which was too take many months. In addition, there was severe damage to the shafts' linings, huge voids caused by the blast and water had to be filled in and made safe. It was to be over twelve months before the remains of the victims started to be recovered, and that is all they were: remains. The intense heat of the fires and explosions reduced the bodies of the victims to mere charred bones. Many of these were found at the foot of the upcast shaft, washed out of the Nine Foot Mine, it was presumed, by the water. Identification of all was considered impossible, but some were able to be recognised. Not in the normal sense though, for they were too mutilated for that. One victim was identified by his clogs by a witness, for the clogs formerly belonged to him. Elizabeth Shuttleworth had the harrowing experience of identifying her husband, killed in the second explosion, by a shoe and a piece of shirt. It was getting on for two years after the disaster, before it was considered that all the remains were recovered. The shafts were then

Pit sinkers in a hoppet. www.cmhrc.co.uk

Oblique aerial view of Moss Colliery. Alan Davies

sealed, and it is credit to the colliery owners that no expense was spared in recovering the bodies and doing the decent thing. All mining disasters are horrific and the Wigan area at that time was no stranger to them. But the Moss Pit Disaster must rank among the most tragic, whilst not in terms of numbers killed, but in the events that occurred afterwards. In Ince Cemetery, a simple memorial records that disastrous day in September 1871, placed there by Thomas Knowles MP one of the owners of the Ince Moss Colliery. The total number of those killed at the Moss Pit was put at seventy men and boys, all but two of them listed below:

Aitkins, James, 20, drawer
Archer, George, 15, drawer
Archer, John, 19, drawer
Archer, Samuel, 21, collier
Banks, William, 18, drawer
Bolton, Charles, 25, collier
Brown, James, 23, collier
Burns, John, 21, drawer
Butler, Michael, 32, sinker
Catterall, Adam, 4, fireman
Dyson, John, 20, drawer
Eddy, John, 28, sinker

Ellison, Thomas, 22, sinker
Finch, John, 19, drawer
Finch, Joseph, 25, collier
Finch, Thomas, 51, collier
Finch, William, 51, collier
Finch, William, junr, 22, drawer
Grady, Michael, 40, hooker-on
Green, George, 30, collier
Greenall, John, 25, collier
Grogan, Patrick, 23, sinker
Harris, James, 22, collier
Hart, Thomas, 25, drawer

Hartley, Robert, 27, drawer
Hasledon, Robert, 38, collier
Heaton, William, 27, collier
Holland, John, 33, collier
Jones, James, 20, drawer
Kelly, John, 16, winder-up
Knowles, John, 50, metalman
Mason, David, 19, drawer
McCue, Patrick, 29, labourer
McKirnel, James, 25, sinker
Morgan, Cutos, 14, drawer
Morgan, William, 33, collier
O'Brian, William, 33, sinker
O'Donohoe, Patrick, 37, collier
Parkinson, George, 22, drawer
Pilkington, George, 32, collier
Pilkington, John, 22, collier
Prescot, Thomas, 18, drawer
Prescott, George, 40, fireman
Radcliffe, Henry, 22, drawer
Reed, James, 26, collier
Richards, Isaac, 21, collier
Richardson, Martin, 19, drawer
Rigby, Henry, 31, collier
Rigby, Thomas ,27, drawer
Shawcross, James, 22, collier
Sheriden, Owen, 25, collier
Smith, William, 24, collier
Swift, William, 35, collier
Taylor, George, 15, drawer
Taylor, John, 25, collier
Taylor, Thomas, 46, collier
Tinsley, Thomas, 17, drawer
Walsh, John, 17, drawer
Walsh, Thomas, 15, drawer
Whaley, John, 31, drawer
White, John, 18, drawer
White, Samuel, 44, drawer
Williams, Thomas, 24, sinker
Winrow, James, 47, metalman
Winstanley, John, 17, drawer
Wood, John, 44, fireman
Wright, William, 12, drawer

This memorial stands in Ince cemetery and recalls the fateful day of the disaster at Moss Colliery, in 1871. The author

New shaft sinkings were made at the colliery and, eventually, another four shafts were working. By the late 1940s Moss was employing nearly 750 men, and was worked by the Wigan Coal Corporation. After nationalisation in 1947 the Coal Board continued mining there until November 1962, when Moss Colliery was eventually abandoned forever, leaving the subterranean workings to its ghosts and its violent past. The events of that fateful September day of 1871 faded away into coal mining history, as yet another disaster that told of the terrible and very real cost of coal in terms of human life.

(23) Saw Mill Pit, Ince in Makerfield: 18 July 1874

The pit bank was filled with anxious relatives waiting for news ...

The Saw Mill Pit, as its name suggests was besides the saw mill and workshops of the Ince Hall Coal and Cannel Company's works at Ince in Makerfield. The pit, which was sunk in 1869, was located behind today's Council Offices on Green Lane and near to the Ince Forge. Saw Mill was sunk to work the Wigan Five Foot at a depth of 363 yards, the Wigan Four Feet Seam, at 391 yards, and the Wigan Six Feet Seam at 416 yards. Close by was the upcast and downcast of what was known as the Pemberton Mines, where the return air from the Saw Mills Pit was extracted; the Saw Mill Pit itself being downcast as for ventilation.

On the Saturday evening, 18 July 1874, the men usually employed at the Saw Mill Pit were drawn to the surface, with the exception of thirteen men in the Four Feet Seam and Five Feet Seam, which were connected by an incline, and twelve men in the Six Feet Seam. Included in the latter was a fireman named John Crompton whose duty it was to fire the shots made previously by the colliers. The others with him were his assistant, nine day workers and the furnace man, making

Once again crowds gather at the pit-head to seek information on loved ones below ground at Saw Mill Colliery in 1874. This print from the Illustrated London News, *3 August 1892, depicts a scene which would have been common in the coalfields of Victorian Britain.* www.cmhrc.co.uk

up the twelve in the Six Feet Seam. At a quarter to seven that Saturday night, there was a loud report from the workings of the mine, followed by a dense cloud of dust at the shaft – once again the population of the Wigan district of Lancashire knew they would soon be grieving for lost souls.

Ten of the men in the Four Feet Mine, having felt the explosion and, being a considerable distance away from the shaft, decided to make their way out by means of what was known as the East Cannel Pit, and were drawn to safety. Exploration parties were quickly formed at the surface, with no lack of volunteers, and they descended the pit shaft. They soon came across the remains of three of the workmen in the Four Feet Mine, who had not been as fortunate as their companions. They had been working nearer the pit shaft, and had felt the full force of the explosion. Two of the three were dead, one of whom was fearfully mangled beyond recognition; the other so dreadfully injured that he died soon after being taken to his home. The searchers pressed on. In the Six Feet Seam two more dead bodies were found; one, a labourer, was discovered seated in a cabin, head in hands, as if accepting his fate. Examination of the workings beyond here was impossible as the afterdamp was too thick to support life so the searchers had to retreat back to the surface. Here, George Gilroy who was manager of the pits in this area took charge of the operations. In a very short time other management and officials of the neighbouring collieries were at hand to give advice and work out the next phase of the exploration. These included Mr C G Jackson of the Wigan Coal and Iron Company, William Bryham junior of the Douglas Bank Colliery, John Bryham of the Rose Bridge Colliery, W H Warbottle of the Walthew House Colliery and John Gerrard, the assistant Mines Inspector for the South Lancashire District.

By the time the Government Inspector arrived at ten o'clock the following morning an exploration party was just emerging from the smouldering mine. They informed him that there might be a fire at some point in the pit, and that all attempts to move forward had been thwarted due to thick smoke and afterdamp. There was also a large fall of roof that impeded progress, and this would have to be removed. They were also of the opinion that there could now be little hope of finding any of the ten remaining missing men alive; it would now be a case of simply finding their bodies, and removing them from the pit. Another consultation was held between the experienced gentlemen, which now included Mr Pickard, the miners' agent. The return air was then examined for any trace of burning, and it was thought that this was not the case. However, when a small party descended the pit at around mid-day, they returned to say that there was a strong smell of fire in the pit. Late afternoon saw another party descend the pit, consisting of Mr Bullen, Mr Beatty, Mr Crippen, Mr Pickard and others. Progress was painfully slow, and continued throughout the night. By eleven o'clock the following Monday morning, the bodies of two of the firemen, John Crompton and Samuel McAlister were brought to the pit bank, terribly disfigured and relatives had a great deal of difficulty identifying them. The men had been found near the place where the shots were fired. The pit bank was filled with anxious relatives waiting for news, and yet there was no sense of excitement – all stood quiet and orderly, waiting for word of those below.

Families and friends wait throughout the night for news at Alexandra Colliery, December, 1875. From the Illustrated London News. www.cmhrc.co.uk

Further into the mine the searchers moved, still hampered by falls of roof, after-damp and methane gas released by the falls, and the threat of further explosions which was very real, but they pressed on, looking for their dead comrades.

The inquest on the seven bodies removed was held soon after, in order to identify the men, and enable the coroner to give certificates for burial. George Gilroy was able to state that they would get three of the other bodies out of the pit later that day, but the other five were thought to be under heavy falls of roof. Three of these were thought to have been working at the chain wheel, which had been thrown over by the heavy falls of roof. The wheel itself was a great weight, and would take at least five men to lift it. Eventually, the Saw Mill Pit reluctantly gave up all its fifteen victims, and they were laid to rest. The damage done to the pit was so bad that it was expected that it would take weeks, perhaps months, to get it back into working order. Those who perished at the Saw Mill Pit, Ince that Saturday evening, were:

John Ashcroft, aged 28, fireman, Newhall Street, Ince, married with two children
John Burns, aged 35, assistant fireman, Hardybutts, Wigan, married with two children
John Harris, aged 54, metalman, Lower Ince, married
Richard Trizise, aged 27, metalman, Lower Ince, married with two children
Richard Rowe, aged 25, metalman, Lower Ince, married with three children
John Crompton, aged 40, fireman, Lower Ince, married with eight children
Samuel M'Alister, fireman, Lower Ince, married with six children
Thomas Shaw, aged 47, bricksetter, Lower Ince, married
John Wood, aged 27, Scholes, Wigan, married with one child
Frank Arthur, aged 50, metalman, Higher Ince, married with five children
Richard Golden, aged 21, labourer, Lower Ince, unmarried
Anthony Jenkins, aged 21, metalman, Higher Ince, unmarried
Oliver Spencer, aged 18, labourer, Scholes, Wigan, unmarried
Charles Kimball, aged 25, labourer, Scholes, Wigan
Martin Roak, aged 45, furnace-man, Scholes, Wigan, widower, left two children.

Twenty-seven children were made orphans in the few seconds it took for the explosion to tear through the workings of the Saw Mill Pit, and their mothers were left to lament and grieve the loss of their husbands. The cause of the explosion was attributed to a blown-out shot having ignited the gas. It has been stated that the Wigan District of Lancashire, and the surrounding areas had three females for every male in the population right up to the turn of the twentieth century. Fine for the boys you might think, but this was a direct result of the men folk being wiped out in mining accidents, whether they were such as this, an explosion, or the multitude of individual accidents that took away life in the coal mines of the district. The Saw Mill Pit, with its dark and deathly past was finally abandoned in 1898.

(24) Alexandra Colliery, New Springs: Wigan, 3 December 1875

... all seven men aboard [the cage] *were thrown to their deaths ...*

The Alexandra Colliery was situated between New Springs and Bottling Wood, near Wigan and had only been open 'about six months' at the time of this shaft accident. The mine was worked by the Wigan Coal and Iron Company who had sunk the shaft down to the Pemberton Four Feet Mine at a depth of 269 yards. The shafts here were 19 feet 6 inches in diameter. In December 1875, work was under-way bricking up the archways at the shaft bottom, a contract let to Mr Holden. At six o'clock on Friday evening 3 December 1875, the men working on this project entered the cage and were lowered down to the shaft bottom. Bricks for the arch-work cement and sand being sent, the men commenced their work. At ten o'clock that night the men returned to the surface for their supper as was usual and at ten-thirty entered the cage again to descend. The signal was given to the

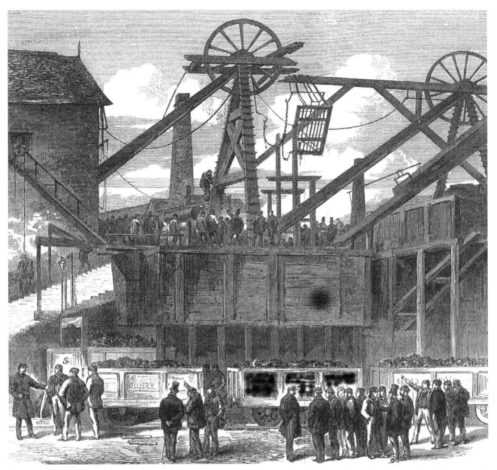

The shattered headgear on the day of the cage disaster may have looked like this. From the Illustrated London News. www.cmhrc.co.uk

engineman, the cage rose slightly and then began to descend the shaft. As the cages met halfway down the pit, by some account they caught each other and all seven men aboard were thrown to their deaths down the shaft. The engineman was aware something was wrong, as the winding ropes went slack followed by a jerk. A number of colliers below heard the commotion and, running to the pit bottom, found that scaffolding over the sump had been smashed. Far below a number of bodies could been seen floating on the surface of the water. A message was quickly sent to Charles Gidlow Jackson, the manager for the Wigan Coal and Iron Company's pits in that area.

He was soon on the spot, and although the guide rods in the shaft, which should have prevented the cages colliding, were twisted and bent, one cage was still operable. Between twelve and one o'clock in the morning, all seven bodies had been recovered and raised to the surface. They were then conveyed to the Packet

House at New Springs to await the coroner's inquest. The cause of the accident was never really determined, and it could only be speculated as to how it happened. Ample room was allowed for the cages to pass each other. Had the guide rods failed for some reason, or were the men improperly balanced, or moving around? This is something we will now never know. Those killed that day in opening out the Alexandra Pit were:

Thomas Bleach, 34, shift chargehand, of Aspull, who left a widow and three children
Patrick Murther, aged 22, labourer, Aspull, unmarried
James Birchall, 26, bricksetter, New Springs, left a widow and two children
Joseph Smith, 20, bricksetter's apprentice, Aspull Moor, unmarried
Joseph Fairclough,19, bricksetter's apprentice, Adlington (lodging at Aspull), unmarried
Charles Holden, 25, metalman, Hindley, married, but with no children
Patrick Nolan, 20, labourer, Wigan, unmarried.

Twenty-odd years after this accident, the Alexandra Colliery employed 548 men and boys underground and 107 surface men. In 1911 there was another accident at the colliery when the whole of the wooden headgearing collapsed around the shaft. The Alexandra Pit was named after the visit to the area by the Prince of Wales and Princess Alexandra in 1873, and was linked with the Lindsay Colliery close by, utilising one of the shafts there as an upcast. Alexandra was abandoned in June 1955, production for the pit's last year being 8,000 tons. Five years previously the pit was working the Ince Seven Feet, and the Ince Six Feet Seams and employed just over 200 men. The surface buildings at the Alexandra Colliery were used for some eight years after it closed in connection with Dairy Pit, situated to the north, beside the Leeds and Liverpool Canal.

(25) Stonehill Colliery, Farnworth: 23 January 1877

Some [men] *were found lying on their faces, their fingers deeply embedded in the earth . . .*

The site of Stonehill Colliery today would be around Bradford Street and Bloomfield Road off the Worsley Road between Farnworth and Walkden. The pit was an old one dating from at least the 1840s, and was abandoned in 1888. A number of seams were worked here including the Yard, Doe, Plodder, Cannel, Trencherbone and Five Quarter. The colliery was worked by Roscow and Lord but following abandonment it was taken over by the Bridgewater Trustees, and utilised as a pumping pit for other collieries in the area. The shaft at the Stonehill Colliery was 300 yards deep and at the time of this accident the underground workings extended a distance of about one mile from the pit bottom.

Three hundred men and boys were at work at the Stonehill Colliery on the morning of Tuesday 23 January 1877 when the alarm was raised that the Cannel Mine at the pit was on fire. A rush was made by those below ground for the shaft. It was later discovered that around 1,200 yards from the pit bottom a wall of Cannel coal over 100 yards in length was alight, the dense fumes and smoke from the fire being carried further into the mine by the ventilation current. The greater part of the men underground that day had managed to escape, but it was known

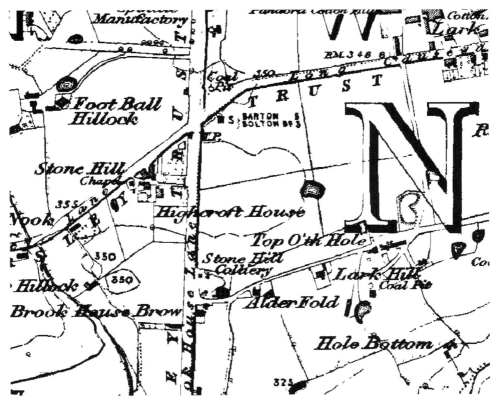

There are no known images of Stonehill Colliery but the pit is marked on the 1844–48 OS map.
Courtesy of Ordnance Survey

that a number of men and boys, up to forty, were still in the pit, and beyond the place where the fire had started. Gas (methane) was virtually unknown in any of the seams worked at the colliery, consequently naked flames, from candles, were allowed to be used by the men.

A number of men beyond the fire soon realised the circumstances and, alarmed by the smoke, made a dash through and managed to escape the sulphurous fumes. They were nearer the fire, but beyond them deeper into the workings 400 yards away were eighteen men and boys, all of whom were believed to have perished. One, who escaped, a man named Bye, stated that he had to pass over seven or eight bodies. He tried to rouse one of the men but failed to make any impression, and presumed that he was dead. Another, named Gerard, with some difficulty passed through the fire when he missed his son. He turned back through the flames, and both were overcome. They presented a pitiful sight when later found clasped in each other's arms in a last embrace. One man named Lindsay battled manfully through the smoke for some distance, but fell to the ground helpless. He had given up all hope of being saved, when he heard voices and, with super-human effort, crawled another 20 yards, and was saved. His companion with him when he fell was among those who succumbed.

Once the fire was reported an exploration party consisting of some twenty men, headed by the manager of the pit, Mr Mills and Mr Bowker, manager of the Bridgewater Trustees, descended the pit. It was decided to lay pipes from the shaft, and try and tackle the flames with water; however, due to the great length that had to be laid, it was not until seven o'clock that night that the job was completed. There was a plentiful supply of water and the fire brigade of the Farnworth Local Board was at hand, as were the hoses and pipes belonging to Messrs Barnes and Holden. It was soon hoped that the flames would be put out and the task of recovering the bodies of the dead men and boys could be continued. On the surface thousands gathered, eager for news of those below, consisting of wives, mothers, sons and daughters, presenting a pitiful and mournful sight. For over three hours the water was poured into the place of the conflagration, with little effect.

A second branch pipe was attached to the hoses, just as and with great suddenness the flames blew back on the rescuerers. Fortunately, no one was hurt but it was believed that this was caused by a massive roof fall. The recovery of the dead was not going to be easy. Throughout the night water was pumped underground and poured onto the flames, but with negative effect. The heat now was so fierce, that it was impossible to get within 80 yards of the flames. An attempt was made to flood part of the pit, thousands of gallons pumped in, but it was found that the water was simply running into some of the lower workings. Some of the rescuers tried entering the place wearing a new device, the Sinclair patent respirator, shaped rather like a diver's helmet, but these proved useless and leaked in the smoke. By this time another length of pipe had been laid from the surface, and the plan to flood the workings continued. By ten o'clock the following day, Wednesday 24 January, this was having little effect, the workings where the fire was dipped away for hundreds of yards, and the plan to flood could take several days. The grieving crowd on the surface had diminished somewhat, but still numbered hundreds. Many had given up all hope, but others found some comfort with the others grieving for lost relatives.

A Mr Bentley and the manager of the Bridgewater Trustees, Mr Temmins, both local colliery owners, offered to encase themselves with the Sinclair respirator and try and reach the fire and throw a couple of hoses forward. The respirator again proved useless, and that plan was abandoned. Still, with total disregard for their own safety, and utterly fatigued, the rescuers worked on. The water hoses were operating at a pressure of almost 300 lbs per square inch, constantly bursting, and persons had to be despatched to Bolton for replacements, causing even more delay in fighting the fire. However, by seven o'clock the following night, Thursday 25 January 1877, the searching parties had the satisfaction in announcing that the fire had been extinguished. The smoke was now disappearing from the workings, but the problem now was the large volumes of steam being given off the still hot coal, an indication of the intense heat in the locality of the fire. It was considered best to keep pouring water for several more hours in order to cool the area, and to prevent further outbreaks of fire. It would not be necessary to pump the workings dry after this, for the area involved could be reached by another airway. Ironically, had those who perished chosen to use this route, then in all probability they would have survived. They appear to have lost all presence of mind and sought the quickest route, that of access to the wagon road, which they used every day in travelling to and from the pit shaft. The recovery of the bodies though through this air course was going to be difficult, since its length was 2,000 yards and it was only 4 feet high. On the surface, Mr Lord of Roscow and Lord had the grim task of ordering and preparing eighteen oaken coffins for the unfortunates. That afternoon, Mr Joseph Dickinson, Inspector of Mines and his deputy descended the pit along with an exploring party. They soon came across the horrific spectacle of all eighteen dead men and boys. Fifteen of these were found together. Some knelt on the ground with hands clasped, as if in prayer; others were seated in the wagonway, apparently meeting their fate with composure; and more were found lying on their faces, their fingers deeply embedded in the earth, testifying their desperate but ill-fated efforts they had made trying to get through the suffocating smoke. Mr Dickinson later stated that had they managed to gain another 40 yards, the men would have reached safety. Two others were found within 25 yards of workings that were not affected at all by the smoke, and another was found within 10 yards of what would have been to him a haven of safety. The flow of water into the pit was stopped and by seven o'clock all of the bodies had been conveyed to the pit-eye, placed in tubs and covered in white sheets. The news that the men and boys had been recovered spread rapidly throughout the district; and soon thousands gathered again on the pit bank. In order to quell the excitement the police were obliged to tell the assembled crowd that the deceased would not be brought to the surface until nightfall. The gruesome task of raising the dead was made more so by the heavy rain and thick smog which surrounded the Farnworth district, but was begun at eight o'clock. The dead were brought up in twos and conveyed in silence along the surface tramway at the pit into the colliery yard, thence into the workshop. One hour later all bodies were out. The faces of the deceased presented a pitiful sight, and were much swollen, yet there was not the slightest burn on any – all had died from asphyxia. One poor fellow, a young lad, appeared to have been struck down while trying to put on his shirt as it still hung loose around his arm. Another poor lad, Richard Shorrocks aged fifteen, judging from the expression on his face, had died without pang, and was found in his father's arms. Soon after the names of those who had died at the Stonehill Colliery could be revealed, they were:

John Stones, aged 23, of Daubhill Street, Farnworth
William Churnside, aged 35, of Bridgewater Street, Farnworth
John Gerrard, aged 20, Albert Road, Farnworth
George Gerrard, brother of the above, aged 23, Albert Road, Farnworth
William Entwistle, aged 27, Glyn Street, Farnworth
James William Brown, aged 19, Cross Street, Farnworth
Thomas Barnes, aged 21, Lord's Quarry, Church Lane, Farnworth
Ralph Eckersley, aged 20, Old Hall Street, Kearsley
Owen Williams, aged 35, Cook Street, Farnworth
Daniel Walker, aged 27, Newport Street, Farnworth
Albert Daley, aged 23, Crompton Street, Farnworth
James Henry Shorrocks, aged 37, Southern Street, Little Hulton
Richard Shorrocks, aged 15, Southern Street, Little Hulton

Joseph Farnworth, aged 26, Topping's House, Little Hulton
Joseph James Hall, aged 26, Worsley Road, Little Hulton
James Lomax, aged 19, Topping's House, Little Hulton
Abraham Stott, aged 31, Tyne Bank, Little Hulton
Thomas Smethurst, aged 44, Queen Street, Little Hulton

The earthly remains of the poor unfortunate victims of the Stonehill Colliery Disaster were interred the following Saturday and the following Monday. Seven were buried at the churchyard of St Paul's at Walkden, the coffins being borne by fellow workmen employed at the pit. Others were buried at St James' near Bury, and at St John's Farnworth, and the newly opened cemetery at Farnworth. The body of Daniel Walker was buried at the latter, which had not yet been consecrated, so permission had to be obtained from the Bishop of Manchester. Daniel was buried there at the request of a number of gentlemen who desired to erect a monument to the memory of those who died that day at Stonehill Colliery. I have tried to locate this memorial but to no avail. The cause of all that carnage and loss of life that day at Farnworth was put down to a lad setting fire to some brattice cloth, used to direct the air course underground. In January 1964 a forty-two-year-old miner and his wife had to run out of their £2,800 bungalow in Worsley Road, Farnworth, just seconds before two bedrooms disappeared into a 1,000-foot mineshaft. Furniture and carpets tumbled into the crater and, soon afterwards, the hallway along which Mr and Mrs William Walker McIvor had escaped, tilted dangerously. A geology expert warned of forty more similar shafts in the area, but police refused to reveal where they were because 'We don't want to cause a general scare.' 'The bungalow', the police added, 'had been built in 1926 on the site of the Stonehill Colliery, formerly owned by Messrs Roscoe and Lord, which was closed in the early 1900s.'

(26) Foggs Colliery, Darcy Lever: 7 February 1877

The search parties made their way with difficulty towards the spot where their unfortunate companions were thought to have been working.

The Farnworth district had barely got over the shock of the Stonehill Colliery Disaster when the area was to be hit once again by another mining tragedy. Foggs Colliery was an old coal mine, it had already been abandoned as the Yard Mine back in 1838. Andrew Knowles and Sons, who owned a number of other pits in the area, such as Agecroft, Clifton Hall, Clifton Moss and the Farnworth Bridge Collieries which were just down the canal from Foggs Pit, also worked and owned Foggs.

There were a number of 'coal pits' around this area of the Manchester, Bolton and Bury Canal at this time, and its difficult to decide just which was the Foggs Pit. It's probably the one marked 'Knowles coal pit' on the map of 1850 on the eastern bank of the canal, north of Hall Lane, on the site later taken by the Hall Chemical Works. This is reinforced by the fact that close by were Foggs Cottages and Farm a few hundred yards further long the canal. 'Knowles coal pit' then would have been on the left hand side of where today stand the Little Lever Comprehensive School. All the rest of this land today is open space and leads on to the Moses Gate

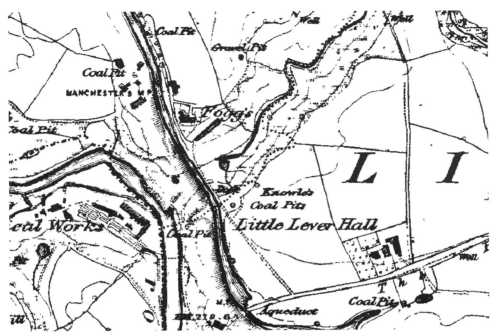

The location of Foggs Colliery, from the OS map of 1844–48. Courtesy of Ordnance Survey

Country Park. The shaft at the Foggs Colliery was 380 yards deep down to the Yard Mine, sometimes known as the Arley Mine, however this was worked out. The upcast shaft for the workings was probably the Victoria Pit to the north west of Darcy Lever Old Hall. At the time of this accident work was going on mining the coal from the Doe Seam, or Seven Feet Mine at a depth of 320 yards in the shaft. Below this, 60 yards deeper were the exhausted workings of the Yard Mine.

Fifty men and boys were employed at the colliery, and the remotest workings were some 900 yards away from the shaft towards Little Lever, Bolton. Naked candles were used by the men, and blasting was carried out, as gas was rarely noted, and the system of ventilation was good. Thirteen men were at work in the remoter district of the mine said to have been underneath the farm of James Edge at Little Lever. The men had been at work a number of hours when, about ten o'clock on 7 February 1877, the surface workers were alarmed by a sudden burst of thick black smoke rising from the Victoria or upcast shaft. There was no loud bang usually associated with colliery explosions, but soon after the signal was received from those below, at the downcast shaft, to be wound up. The men and boys were quickly raised, the last being Absalom Norris, the underviewer. One and all reported that their workings had filled up with smoke, but no-one was sure whether this was the result of a fire or an explosion. Two of the men raised up the pit, Thomas Hindley and James Hurst were among the men working under James Edge's farm, and said that they were alarmed by a sudden rush of smoke into the workings, and therefore took to their heels. So thick was the smoke, that they had no time to warn their fellow workmen, but if they had turned back, even for a few moments they felt they would have been suffocated. Afterdamp followed them for a distance of 250 yards and, when they did reach the shaft, they were suffering greatly from the effects of the gas. A roll-call was taken of all the men in the pit that day, and it was found that ten of their number were unaccounted for. Norris, the underviewer, and practically all the men, at once descended the shaft again in search of their comrades. The search parties made their way with difficulty towards the spot where their unfortunate companions were thought to have been working.

It was evident that there had indeed been an explosion for in places the roof had fallen in; and in other areas air stoppings had been blasted down, and smoke filled the subterranean workings, in what was now a quiet and almost eerie atmosphere. Despair struck the would-be rescuers when it was discovered that the explosion had ignited the coal, cutting off all hope of escape of anyone who might have survived the initial blast. Still, courageous attempts were made to force a way through the thick smoke, but it was all in vain. The men were eventually forced to retreat back to the shaft, many suffering from the effects of the thick smoke. On the surface communication had been sent to Peter Howcroft, the manager to Messrs Knowles and Co, and the information was also reaching the neighbouring collieries of the Bridgewater Trustees and Fletcher and Sons. Their managers and other volunteers were soon at the scene of the catastrophe, offering advice and helping hands. A growing band of relatives also gathered on the pit top waiting for news, the women mourning, old men with tears in their eyes, all hoping, perhaps beyond hope that those below could be recovered alive. Further explora-

Miners and rescue workers struggle forward in search of their comrades following the explosion at Foggs Colliery, December 1877, a scene typified in this image from the Illustrated London News, 2 *August 1878.* www.cmhrc.co.uk

tion parties were formed, and several of their number were provided with the 'Sinclair' helmet respirators. A number of the men were assigned to removing the debris brought down by the explosion, others spragged the shattered roof of the mine. Measures were also taken to restore the current of air to try and clear the smoke. Bricks and mortar to rebuild the stoppings were being sent down the pit in every available cage and, in between, more and more volunteers descended, as exhausted rescue workers ascended. Within a few hours, and with applaudable efforts, the searchers had the satisfaction of reporting that for a distance of 800 yards from the shaft bottom all the workings were free of foul air.

There was sad news however for the poor creatures who had gathered on the pit bank, making anxious enquiries of loved ones, of missing husbands, fathers, brothers and sons, for beyond the 800 yards it was impossible to penetrate further. All beyond that barrier were now, without question, dead. It was now a case of recovering the bodies, not rescuing them. By nine-thirty that night, although not through lack of efforts, the searchers had made just a miserable 60-yards progress forward. Here they discovered the dead body of a pit pony, overcome by suffocating afterdamp. The men too, had to be sent out of the mine in ever increasing numbers, feeling the effects of smoke and foul air. Some were almost insensible through inhaling the afterdamp, and had to be lifted into tubs in the cages. On the surface they were treated by Dr Douglas. They recovered, but were in such a state of exhaustion that they were not allowed back down the pit. By ten o'clock it was thought that the fire was out, but the remoter workings were so full of smoke and afterdamp, that it defied all attempts to penetrate it. To the grieving crowd, the manager of the pit read out the names of those who now were beyond all hope:

Robert Hall, Hall Lane, Farnworth, single
James Berry, Little Lever, married with two children
George Berry, Little Lever, single
James Partington senior, Darcy Lever
Ralph Partington, Darcy Lever
Abraham Lawton, MacDonell Street, Farnworth, married with six children
Aaron Partington, Moor Lane, Bolton
James Partington, son of Ralph Partington
James Holden, Darcy Lever, single
Henry Aspinall, Darcy Lever, married with one child

It was some weeks before all the bodies of the unfortunate victims of the Foggs Colliery Disaster were recovered, and finally laid to rest. With the approval of Joseph Dickinson, the Mines Inspector, the return air course was bricked up but the fire *was* still burning. The following day the other air course was bricked up, thus entirely sealing off the mine. It was only when the fire was finally extinguished that the bodies were taken out. The explosion was thought to have occurred through the gas coming into contact with one of the naked candles used at the pit. The Foggs Pit did reopen after the disaster, and in the mid-1890s employed 198 men and boys underground, and thirty-eight surface workers. Another disaster struck the pit on 4 October 1907 when nine men were killed in a shaft accident. The cage became disconnected with the rope and plunged down

The legacies of coal mining days are still with us. On Christmas Day 2005, a huge gaping hole appeared in the backyard of stable owners Michael and Jennifer Lomax at Darcy Lever near Bolton. The crater was an old mine shaft dating back to the early nineteenth century which had collapsed taking with it a tractor and four large mature sycamore trees. The pit shaft was last worked in 1902, and was capped off in 1978. It was thought that the shaft walling had given way and taken the concrete cap with it. Happily no-one was hurt, and at the time this picture was taken on 4 January 2006 the trees and tractor were perilously perched over a 500 feet drop of the old mine.

past the shaft bottom into some old workings abandoned many years before, which were then flooded, all the men on board drowning. Time was running out for the pit however, and after a long and credible lifetime, the colliery was abandoned forever on 24 November 1913, not long before the start of the Great War. Today, the site of the industrious Foggs Colliery and its dark past, and with its loss of ten men and boys in 1877, is a green open space, a place for leisure rather than toil. How many people, I wonder, while walking their dogs, or strolling along with their children here, know of the valiant efforts of the mine workers, or of those who perished beneath their feet all those years ago?

(27) Unity Brook Pit: 12 March 1877

The scene before them was chaotic, with broken timbers, roof falls and mine tubs.

Unity Brook Colliery was located between Kearsley and Clifton, close by the Unity Brook Farm off the Manchester Road, and a short distance away from the Spindle Point Colliery. In fact Unity Brook, Spindle Point and Manor collieries were in later years interconnected underground. There were two shafts at the Unity Brook Colliery, upcast and downcast in ventilation, the downcast was the one used for the winding of coal and men. The depth of the shafts was about 360 yards down to the Cannel Seam, the other seam worked at the pit was the Trencherbone, some 60 yards above the Cannel Mine. The workings were stated to be of a small extent, which would seem to indicate that these two seams had only just been opened up. From the bottom of the downcast shaft in the Cannel Mine an inclined roadway was driven to the dip of the seam, at approximately 1 in 4 away from the shaft.

This roadway was known as the Engine Plane Down Brow and from here five other roadways on each side were driven to the boundary, the East and the West workings. These in turn were connected at intervals of about 40 yards and various air doors controlled the air currents around the workings of the mine. Open lights (candles) were in use at the colliery and indeed were preferred by the miners over the Davy lamp. This was not unusual in this part of the Lancashire Coalfield at this time, the miners at Clifton Hall Colliery seven years after this disaster were still using candles! This might well be understood, for no gas was ever found at the pit, until September 1877 when the cut-throughs were made at the far end of the workings. Following this however, there were a number of reports of gas at the pit.

The early morning shift at Unity started in the usual manner for the colliery underlooker James Holt on 12 March 1878. He descended the pit to make his pre-shift examination and, at the far end of the West Workings he found a small fall of roof. This he apparently considered of little importance, and in all other respects the colliery workings were as normal. However, in the course of the morning he was called back to the area of the roof fall by his assistant William Mayoh. The fall had increased considerably, having come down some 3 or 4 feet in thickness and covering an area of about 10 yards by 7 yards. In addition, the roof was still coming down on the pack walls, which had been built to support it. In these circumstances a man of Holt's experience, and also those of the fireman Mayoh, should have immediately forbidden the use of naked lamps. As this was the first roof fall of its type on these West Workings, they either chose to ignore the matter or it never occurred to them. Holt went to the top of the fallen debris where he found a good circulation of air. He then arranged with fireman Mayoh and some of the men to set a good strong prop before setting off to his other duties. James Holt finished his work in the Cannel Mine and then went up into the Trencherbone Seam some 60 yards above. Here he spent an hour or two seeing to the workings before making his way to the cage due to be wound up about one o'clock in the afternoon. His usual time for getting to the pit top would normally be around three o'clock, but the colliery manager Isaiah Johnson was away for the day on colliery business, and Holt had to see to affairs on the surface. He signalled the cage to be brought from the Cannel Mine. When the cage arrived at the Trencherbone Mouthing in the shaft he found a miner named Ralph Welsby from the East Side workings of the Cannel Mine. It was also before Welsby's time for coming up the pit, but he had arranged beforehand to leave early to see his sick child. The two men emerged on the pit banking, at exactly ten minutes past one o'clock, and it was then that the pit fired. All the men in the Cannel Mine, numbering forty-two, lost their lives as well as the onsetter at the Trencherbone mouthing. Such was the blast, both shafts were dis-arranged, the lining was ripped out of the upper portion, timbers were broken and steel landing plates were torn up. One of the cages at the downcast shaft was at the top and escaped the greater force of the blast through there being an opening at the bottom of it, the other cage was at the bottom of the Cannel Mine.

The rope to this cage hung in the shaft loose and dis-connected. Hurried arrangements were quickly made. James Holt the underlooker, accompanied by two men, one of them named Teesdale, entered the cage. They descended to within 5 yards above the Trencherbone Mine when the cage was stopped by fallen debris. Holt got out of the cage and, clinging to the cage guide ropes, climbed down to the Trencherbone mouthing, here he found several men still alive.

Joseph Dickinson, the Mines Inspector for the area, in response to a telegraph was at the colliery about three o'clock, just two hours after the event. By this time a hoppet had replaced the cage in the shaft, some of the debris had been removed and Holt was able to get some men out of the Trencherbone Mine. The air coming up the shaft smelled strongly of afterdamp, but happily there was no smell of burning which indicated at least that there was no fires below ground. The fresh air was still being drawn down the downcast shaft, though the men being removed smelled the afterdamp and some appeared to be suffering from the effects of the gas. The air going down the shaft to the Trencherbone Mine was soon contaminated with the fumes and afterdamp rising from the Cannel Mine. There was no sign of life from that seam. News spread quickly. A number of mining engineers from other local collieries were on the scene to give their assistance, including Edward Pilkington and Simon Horrocks. About thirty men were raised from the Trencherbone Seam as quickly as possible before there was any change in circumstances, otherwise all would have been lost. The Mines Inspector Joseph Dickinson and underlooker Holt descended to the Trencherbone Mine, where the air current appeared to take its normal course, and was 'downcasting'. The two men made a quick search for the missing onsetter, but were unable to find him. They then checked that the main air doors were intact and that the ventilation furnace was out, and all appeared to be in order. Following this, an attempt was made to descend down to the Cannel Mine but the shaft was blocked solid with timber and other debris. They shouted down through the broken timbers in a vain hope of some reply, but none was forthcoming, and they returned to the surface arranging for the pit carpenters to descend and remove the obstructions. An hour later they returned up the shaft, bringing with them the dead body of the onsetter whom they found in the sump at the bottom of the shaft having been blown there with the blast of the explosion. Holt, Dickinson, a Mr Grimshaw and a Mr Woodward again descended the shaft, and this time they made it to the Cannel Mine. The scene before them was chaotic with broken timbers, roof falls and mine tubs. The air was thick with afterdamp and made the men's eyes water, but enough oxygen was gratefully present to make it breathable. The rescuers first tried to move along the upper west level where the fall had occurred earlier that morning, but found the afterdamp and firedamp too much. Leaving this, they went to the engine brow where they found considerable destruction, and then proceeded through the other parts of the mine as quickly as possible. All the men that they came across in these workings were already dead; their bodies were burnt and some of them were badly injured, nearly all apparently lying where they were struck by the blast. The air doors and screens were all blown away, but the searchers managed to get to all the workings except the upper west levels. Having made sure there was no further life to save, they made their way back

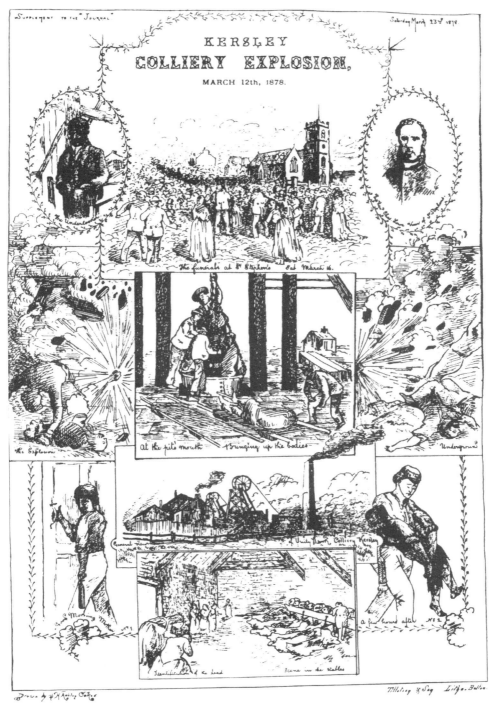

This is how the local newspaper, the Journal *of 23 March 1878 illustrated the disaster at Unity Brook Colliery.* Author's collection

towards the shaft about eight o'clock having explored for some two hours. Arrangements were made to restore the ventilation and remove the rest of the bodies and to protect those doing this work.

By the following day the upcast shaft was explored and found to be damaged like the downcast, with rubble littering the pit shaft bottom having either fallen or been blown there. All the bodies had been found except for three, which were later found under the debris in the sump hole at the bottom of the shaft. It was now possible to reach the fall on the west level workings, and this now extended for some 25 yards by 20 yards, or seven times the extent it was when Holt left it before the explosion. Firedamp was still coming off freely and mixing with the general body of the air. Here the pit was coated with dust and near the fall was a deposit of soot. The fall was determined as the centre of the blast as timber, trams, air doors, wood and steel lay scattered around the workings.

Twelve months later, when Joseph Dickinson again returned to the pit, gas was still issuing from the explosive point from fresh fissures. Nineteen men and boys from this disaster were laid to rest in the churchyard at St Stephen's, Kearsley and 100 widows and fatherless children were left to mourn from this disaster. The jury recorded that the deaths of the deceased was purely accidental and that all possible precautions had been used in the working of the mine. This is in spite of the evidence of Joseph Dickinson's statement: *'That if self-extinguishing lamps, like Stephenson's or the Muizer, been in use at the colliery, the gas would in all probability passed off harmlessly, and forty three men and boys over whom so many households are weeping would have been alive now.'* One writer to the local newspaper, condemning the verdict captured the feelings of many: *'Safety lamps were not used because it was resolved after due deliberation, that money is more precious than human life.'* The weeping wives and mothers of the time would I am sure have agreed.

Rather like the proverbial *'Closing the door after the horse has bolted'* naked flames were never again used at Unity Brook Colliery. The Doe, Trencherbone, Five Quarters and Cannel Mines were abandoned at Unity Brook Colliery in May 1881. There appears to no permanent memorial to the disaster here.

Those who perished were:

Alfred Isherwood, aged 32	Andrew Walker, aged 22
James Byrom, aged 32	Wright Lomax, aged 26
Thomas Byrom, aged 28	George Booth, aged 21
John Tickle Lomax, aged 31	John Haynes, aged 21
John Hamblet, aged 31	James Beattie, aged 19
George Jackson, aged 28	Thomas Peake, aged 17
Amos Lomax, aged 17	Thomas Hilton, aged 20
Thomas Mace, aged 19	William Leach, aged 24
Joseph Welsby, aged 18	George Lindley, aged 47
John Greenhalgh, aged 26	Ellis Lord (Lindley), aged 15
James Partington, aged 44	William Morris, aged 15
Joseph Hobson, aged 26	John Harrison, aged 40
Robert Enion, aged 39	Charles Tong, aged 16
Samuel Wolstenholme, aged 47	Richard Featherstone, aged 18
Thomas Lever, aged 18	Robert Clarke, aged 18

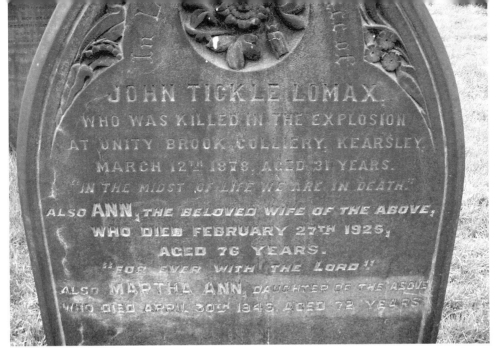

The grave of John Tickle Lomax who was killed at the Unity Brook Colliery, St Stephen's churchyard, Kearsley Moor. The author

Richard Wallwork, aged 25
Peter Fogg, aged 26
James Hobson
James Chadwick, aged 38
David Enion, aged 13
William Wolstenholme, aged 21
Absolom Barnes, aged 14

William Barnes, aged 38
Thomas Lomax, aged 28
Thomas Wolstenholme, aged 41
Christopher Moore, aged 26
Jonathan Enion, aged 12
William Mayon, aged 33

The grave of John Tickle Lomax can be seen at the church of St Stephen's Kearsley Moor, and bears the following inscription: '*John Tickle Lomax, who was killed at the Unity Brook Colliery, Kearsley, March 12 1878, aged 31 years.*'

(28) King Pit, Pemberton Colliery, Pemberton: 11 October 1877

How the little village of Pemberton must have grieved and mourned.

The year 1877 was a disastrous one for coal mining in Lancashire terminating in October with an explosion at the King Pit of the Pemberton Colliery. The Pemberton Colliery consisted of the Queen Pit, King Pit, Prince Pit and an old Bye Pit; and was begun by the Blundell Family from 1815 through to 1827, with other sinkings at various dates. A person named Hollinshead Blundell was working the pit in 1834, according to a directory; however, the pits will always be associated with Jonathan Blundell and Sons. The pits were situated between Foundry Lane and Little Lane near the Pemberton Railway Station, off the Billinge Road at Pemberton. The first sods of the Queen and King Pits were cut on 2 December 1867 with the intention of winning the Wigan Seams, the King Coal, Orrell Five Feet Seam, Arley Seam, and the Cannel Coal. The downcast shaft at the colliery was the

Queen Pit, 17 feet in diameter, and the upcast shaft the King Pit, 19 feet in diameter, both 640 yards deep. From the King Pit the Four Feet Seam was won at a depth of 270 yards, the Nine Feet at 300 yards, and the King and Cannel at a depth of 364 yards. At the Queen Pit, the Orrell Four Feet and Five Feet were wound. Both shafts were linked for ventilation purposes. This was achieved by a massive Guibal fan 46 feet in diameter and 15 feet wide driven by a steam engine, with a duplicate in case of breakdown. At the top of the fan drift an escape chimney was fitted and provided with four large doors, so that in case of an explosion the blast would pass through without doing damage to the fan.

It was here on Thursday afternoon, at one o'clock on 11 October 1877, that the first signs of the explosion was noticed, as huge volumes of dust, smoke were seen rising from the pit. Soon signals were received from below and, in quick succession, the cage was lowered and raised as the information was given that an explosion had taken place in the Nine Feet Seam. An exploring party was soon arranged consisting of Mr Watkin, the colliery manager, Mr Cook, certificated manager, Mr R Laverick, the underlooker for the King Pit, Messrs Crossley and A E Wood, surveyors George Ashurst, Joseph Simpkin, William Stephens and others. Meanwhile all the other men and boys, totalling some 600 working in the other seams of the mine, were drawn to the surface and work was stopped. At the Queen Pit progress was impossible as the air doors and brattice were blown down, the ventilation interrupted, the exploration stopped by large amounts of after-damp. A descent was then made at the King Pit, not the normal mode of exploration, as here the fan would draw the afterdamp. The worst fears were realised

The scene at Pemberton Colliery on the day of the disaster. From the Illustrated London News, *20 October 1877.* www.cmhrc.co.uk

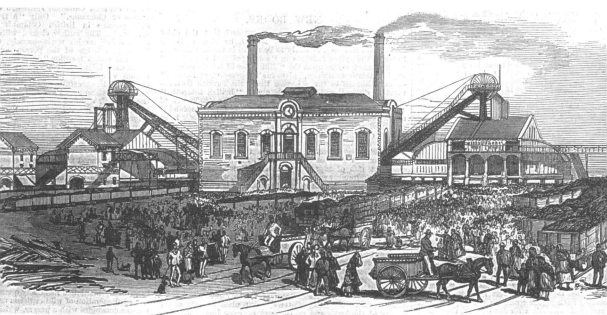

here, it was utter devastation, timbers were broken, tubs overturned, and any progress into the far workings was stopped by the afterdamp. The tunnel connecting the two shafts was cleared, and the ventilation restored in that section, but so powerful was the afterdamp, that any lengthy stay underground was impossible. Shortly after two o'clock W J L Watkin, the manager, R P Cook, underground manager and Robert Laverick decided to try and enter the workings in the hope of finding some of the men alive – the other searchers were left behind. After some time the waiting men became alarmed since they had not heard from the leaders in front for a number of minutes. They set off to try and find them and, at a jig brow about 200 yards from the mouth to the workings, and 100 yards from the main airway, they were horrified to find the managers lying on the floor of the pit unconscious.

Cook was foremost, with the other two a short distance behind – they had evidently become aware of the danger, and tried to escape the afterdamp, only to be overtaken. The bodies were quickly taken into the fresher air, and communication was sent above ground for assistance. Surgeons Barnes, Johnstone and Hartley agreed to go and help. At first sight the three victims appeared to be dead, but nevertheless artificial respiration was administered, but to no avail and the men were pronounced as deceased. On the surface of the mine, as usual, large crowds had gathered to await information of loved ones from below. Between half-past five and six o'clock the bodies of Cook, Watkin and Laverick were wound slowly to the surface at the Pemberton Colliery. Deprived of the chief members of management, the workmen appeared paralysed, and word had to be sent out to other collieries for assistance in recovering the rest of the men and boys, all of whom were now presumed to be dead. Soon, a number of engineers were at hand, including George Holland of the Winstanley Collieries – they began their grim task in earnest.

Amazingly, a number of survivors were wound up from the Nine Feet Mine, including Peter and Joseph Heaton, William Greaves, William Murray and James Allerton, all pony lads. All were suffering to one extent or another from the afterdamp, and soon removed to their homes. Another incident at this time was one of the most remarkable in the annals of coal mining history. John Allerton was working in the pit when the disaster struck, and was picked by the force of the explosion and drove with hellish force into the woodwork of the shaft, and there entangled. Here he lay with nothing more than a broken arm suspended over the void below him until rescued some time later. When questioned about the accident he said 'For a time after the explosion I knew nothing, as I was partially stunned. When I came to myself a bit, I felt my wrist aching and my feet off the ground. I was in total darkness and, I may add, despair, for I instinctively felt that I was hanging in the shaft. I was afraid to move, for fear that the woodwork that held my wrist in its grip would give way. I can tell you that I was thankful to God when I saw the glimmer of the lights of the safety lamps carried by the rescue men. They soon had me in a safer grip. In a twinkling they had me in their arms, and – here I am.'

Below ground, work continued in trying to restore the ventilation of the mine, a task that went on until the late evening. As the workings were opened up, a fire

BRINGING UP THE DEAD

Bringing the dead up from the mine workings at Pemberton Colliery, Illustrated London News, *20 October 1877.* www.cmhrc.co.uk

was discovered, and once again the men had to be withdrawn, and consultations were entered into with the engineers. It was decided that a small exploration party should descend the pit and assess the situation. These explorers returned about midnight. Following their report, it was decided that an attempt would be made brick off that section of the mine where the fire was burning. Bands of volunteers moved forward, and the task in hand proceeded with vigour. Working in terrible conditions, these bands of willing helpers had to be replaced at regular intervals, as each group became exhausted, overcome with the heat and bad air. By ten o'clock the following day the task was completed and, following another consultation, it was decided that the other airway would have to be bricked up too, thus completely depriving oxygen to the flames. This done, work was once again begun on restoring the normal air course to the general workings of the pit. Eventually, the fire was extinguished and the forbidding task of recovering those who had perished was begun. By seven o'clock the following Sunday, the greater part of the workings had been explored, and the heart rending recovery of twenty-six of their colleges had been completed. Seven others were still missing but were soon found, making a total, including the three searchers who died, of thirty-six men and boys. This is the official figure; however, the list below includes thirty-seven lives. The dead were placed in a workshop on the surface of the pit and, following an inspection by a jury, permission was granted for burials. Those who perished at the Pemberton Colliery were named as:

Mr W. J. L. Watkin, aged 36, manager of the Pemberton Colliery of Wood Cottage, Pemberton, married but no family

Mr R. P. Cook, aged 46, underground manager, Pemberton, married with seven daughters, the youngest being 14 years of age

Robert Laverick, aged 39, Highfield, Pemberton, married with three children, the youngest five years old

Identifying those killed at Pemberton Colliery, and the harrowing scenes in the temporary mortuary,
Illustrated London News, *20 October 1877.* www.cmhrc.co.uk

James Winstanley, a drawer of Orrell, not married

James Taylor, aged 45, a fireman, married with five children, the youngest being five
years of age

Nicholas Halliwell, aged 30, overman, married with three children

Luke Parkinson, a collier of Goose Green, married with one child

William Byrom, aged 14, pony driver of Wosley Mesnes

Edward Birch, aged 13, pony driver of Newtown

Matthew Preston, aged 13, pony driver, Lambert Head Green

Robert Ritchie, aged 27, hooker-on, Pemberton, single

John Woodcock, aged 24, drawer, of Worsley Mesnes, married with two children, the
youngest being just 15 weeks old

Robert Pemberton, single in lodgings

John Kelly, drawer

Thomas Roby, drawer, of Newtown, married

James Murray, aged 24, drawer, of Goose Green, married, no children

William Heaton, aged 21, drawer, Halfway House, Pemberton, single

Richard Taberner, aged 16, drawer, of Scotch Lane, Newtown

Charles Beedel, aged 13, pony driver, Goose Green

Peter Charnock, aged 17, drawer, of Goose Green

Benjamin Hartley, aged 24, drawer, of Newtown, single

Frank Higgins, aged 24, drawer of Thwaites Delf, single

Luke Taylor, aged 19, drawer, Little Lane, brother to James Taylor above

John Kellett, collier, Alexandra Terrace, Pemberton, single

John Bradshaw, collier, halfway House, married with three children, youngest
12 months

William Hulme, aged 49, collier, Newtown, married with one son, eight years of age

Daniel Price, aged 32, left a wife and two children

John Atherton, collier of Lamberhead Green, married with five children

Screening (cleaning) coal was often carried out by women workers in the South Lancashire Coalfield. This is a scene typical of the screening process that would have taken place at Pemberton Colliery. From the Illustrated London News, *12 October 1878.* www.cmhrc.co.uk

William Chapman, Colliery of Pemberton, married with five children, youngest two years old

John Cubbins, collier, Pemberton, left a wife and two children

Thomas Steadman, collier, Newtown, married with two children

George Rutter, collier, Pemberton, married with five children

Patrick Broadie, collier, of Pemberton, age unknown

John Wood, aged 31, collier, Pemberton

John Wild, collier, Lamberhead Green, married

Thomas Rudd, collier, age unknown

William Webb, aged 24, drawer of Newtown, married with one child

The cause of the Pemberton Colliery Disaster was attributed to an ignition of firedamp, ignited by shotfiring. These repeated and terrible colliery disasters led to the formation in 1873 of the Lancashire and Cheshire Miners' Permanent Relief Society. Its main aim was to provide for the unfortunate wives and children of miners lost in disasters such as the above, and the many others that were to follow. The money in this case was handed out at the colliery school. Colonel Blundell, the owner of the Pemberton Colliery, supplemented the funeral costs, by donating 25 per cent of the amount paid to the women and children by the Society. Imagine the pitiful scenes in the following days as funeral followed funeral when each of the poor men and boys were laid to rest. How the little village of Pemberton must have grieved and mourned. The colliery did recover, and had a fine and profitable life. By the 1920s, the Pemberton Pits were being worked by the Pemberton Colliery Company Ltd, and a decade later was employing 1,365 men underground and 473 surface workers. The Pemberton Collieries were abandoned on 3 November 1946, and are described as 'pumping only' in 1948. Today, Pemberton Colliery is a fifty-acre reclaimed mine site and is being developed as a manufacturing and distribution park.

(29) Alexandra Colliery, Thatto Heath: 22 October 1879

The engine continued to ascend, now at a greater speed, until it smashed into the wooden headgear.

The Alexandra Colliery was located between the railway and Crossley Road to the north of Thatto Heath, south of St Helens, Lancashire. The pit dated from 1867, when sunk by Pilkington Brothers, the famous glassmakers. The pit was so named on account of a royal visit by Princess Alexandra during the sinking of the mine. Alexandra Drive running up besides the Ravenhead Works of the Pilkington Glass Company also recalls this event. In later years the colliery was linked to the Ravenhead Pit, and worked under the title of St Helens Collieries Company Limited. In 1945 over 1,000 men were employed. By the time the pits were nationalised in January 1947, the Alexandra Pit had become the ventilation and pumping shaft for the Ravenhead Colliery. Working under the National Coal Board, the Ravenhead Colliery was producing 306,000 tons per annum in 1956, and employed 1,043 men underground.

The Alexandra Colliery's dubious claim to fame was a winding accident on Wednesday 22 October 1879, when seven men were plunged to the bottom of the

400 yard deep shaft. This was caused quite simply by the 'forgetfulness' of the shaft engine winder.

The men at the pit were going about their normal duties at the usual hour of six o'clock in the morning, and several cage loads of miners had already descended the pit. Nine more entered the cage for the descent and the signal was given to lower the cage by the banksman, the person in charge at the top of the shaft. The gearing on the steam engine however, had not been changed into reverse mode, and the cage began to rise up into the winding wheels of the headstocks. One man and a youth, seeing the danger, leapt out of the cage, one of them getting injured slightly, and the other more so, but nothing compared to what would happen to their companions. The engine continued to ascend, now at a greater speed, until it smashed into the heavy balk of the wooden headgear. The winding rope then broke and the cage, being liberated, fell with a fearful crash into the depths of the pit, carrying with it the seven unfortunate occupants. The cage was, of course, smashed to pieces, and those onboard fearfully mutilated. As efforts to recover the bodies were being made, headed by the colliery manager, Mr France, the pit top soon became crowded with anxious friends and grieving relatives eager for news of those who had perished below. It was stated that Joseph Naylor, the engine winder, had been at the colliery for twenty years. Those who were killed in the shaft were named as:

Peter Aspinall, aged 32, collier
Henry Norton, aged 30, collier
William Parr, aged 50, collier
Thomas Kay, aged 45, collier
James Webster, aged 38, collier
Joseph Holland, aged 28, drawer
David Dixon, aged 16, drawer

By 1968, the Ravenhead Colliery that was connected with the ill-fated Alexandra Colliery, was employing 354 men underground and 139 surface workers, mining from the Wigan Four Feet and Arley Mines. This was the last time the pit was mentioned in the *Guide to the Coalfields* and must have closed soon after. The Ravenhead Nature Park was built on the site of muckstack of the former Ravenhead Colliery, the spoil being used for the building of a section of the M6, and the site used for landfill in the late 1980s. The full restoration of the colliery site took place between 1993 and 1996.

(30) Shakerley Colliery, Tyldesley: 2 October 1883

Barely had the cage gone out of sight of daylight, when one of the coupling chains on top snapped …

There were two Shakerley Pits, one worked by the Tyldesley Colliery Company, the other by William Ramsden. This shaft accident occurred at William Ramsden's Nelson Pit at the Shakerley Colliery. William Ramsden's Pit was located on Shakerley Road at Tyldesley. The other 'Shakerley Pit' was to the west of Cleworth Hall Colliery along Cleworth Hall Road. Mr Ramsden and his grandfather had worked the Shakerley Colliery since 1839 and the pit was relatively free of accidents until this one. There is earlier evidence however of Shakerley Colliery since it is recorded that a John Hope, who died at Chaddock in 1798, had an interest in the mine. This he left to his son, also named John, and to his son-in-law, Thomas Smith. It is probable that the Ramsdens purchased the pit from them. The Wellington Pit at Shakerley Colliery was sunk in 1866, and the Nelson Pit in 1869, both named after our famous heroes.

At just after six o'clock on 2 October 1883 most of the men at the Nelson Pit, Shakerley Colliery, had descended to start their day's work. The pit was sunk down to the Trencherbone Mine at a depth of 280 yards. Six men entered the cage and the signal was given to lower them into the pit. The cage lifted slightly in order to let the banksman remove the keps, which held the cage steady at the top, and then the cage started off into the depths of the shaft. Barely had it gone out of sight of daylight, when one of the coupling chains on top snapped and the cage and its human freight plunged down the pit. Those at the bottom, on hearing the cage crashing downwards, ran for cover as it ploughed through the thick balks of timber covering the watery sump. There was not the slightest hope of any of its occupants having survived. All that remained to do was get the bodies out and back onto the surface. James Berwick, the colliery manager, headed this operation. By eight o'clock four of the poor miners had been recovered, and by twelve o'clock all were out and named as:

> Thomas Aldred, aged 18, of Lee Lane, Tyldesley, single
> William Liversage, Lee Lane, Tyldesley, married with one child
> Ashton Hayes, Lee Lane, Tyldesley, single
> Patrick McGuire, John Street, Tyldesley, married with two children
> Edward Wild, Common Lane, Tyldesley, single
> Jonathan Williams, a youth, Greenbank Street, Tyldesley.

The last mentioned 'youth' was the eldest son of Samuel and Elizabeth Williams, and was only thirteen years old. His younger brother, William also worked at the pit. Another of the deceased, Edward Wild, was a native of Hyde, and he lodged with Alfred Jones at Tyldesley. In the confusion that followed the accident, Alfred Jones' wife was informed that it was her husband who had been killed. Jones worked at the same pit, but had gone down safely in the previous cage. All the victims of the accident were of course dreadfully mutilated. Edward Wild had his arms and legs broken and had several wounds around the head. William Liversage had his neck broken in the crash. A young lad, Samuel Halliwell, worked as a drawer for Patrick McGuire and, in normal circumstances they went down the pit together. Samuel was late that morning, and just missed the cage that McGuire was in, so being late saved his life.

By the turn of the twentieth century the Wellington and Nelson pits of the Shakerley Colliery were employing over 500 men and boys. However, in 1938 the Nelson Pit is listed as abandoned, and just before it had closed employed 129 workers underground, along with one hundred surface workers; and was worked by Manchester Collieries. There was a local saying at Tyldesley that the owners of the Nelson Pit were 'too tight' to have cages in the shaft, and that they would only employ miners with bald heads. Because there were no cages, large rubber plungers were placed on the end of the winding ropes and – well you can guess the rest!

(31) Clifton Hall Colliery, Pendleton, Manchester: 18 June 1885

… the men seemed to have been struck dead, some at work and some at breakfast.

You would have to look hard and long to find a memorial or evidence of this terrible colliery disaster today; however, for those interested there is a memorial at St Augustine's Church off the Bolton Road at Pendleton. There are also a number of graves in local churches stating that the occupants perished at Clifton Hall Colliery, and bear witness, were it was needed, to the appalling day when 178 men and boys lost their lives in a coal-mining disaster 'just waiting to happen'.

The memorial to the Clifton Hall Colliery Disaster at St Augustin's Church, Bolton Road, Pendlebury. The author

At the inquiry that followed there was a censorious and bitter attack on the general running of the pit, on the management and officials alike. Naked lights were allowed even though gas was known to be present in the mine; rules forbidding matches and tobacco were also never effectively enforced. One of the record books suddenly went missing following the explosion and the fireman who should have made the last entries conveniently 'forgot' how many entries for gas had been recorded that day. The truth was he could not even read or write and someone had to do the entries for him.

An underground tunnel from the Clifton Hall Colliery connected with the nearby Agecroft Colliery was a supposed escape route but suffered from roof falls and at one point was filled with water to within 2 feet of the roof. This space quickly filled with noxious firedamp after the explosion. A number of the men and boys who might have otherwise survived died there, in spite of the very brave attempts of the rescue workers.

Clifton Hall Colliery, the scene of all this devastation, was located on Lumms Lane, off the Agecroft Road at Pendleton, Manchester and, on the surface, was only about 800 yards from Agecroft Colliery, both pits being owned by Andrew Knowles and Sons. Even at a time when coal-masters were generally despised for their lack of interest in the mines they owned and their unwillingness to invest money (but were keen to take the profits at any cost, even at the expense of the safety of the men and boys they employed), this firm was bitterly hated. The Chairman and Managing Director was Andrew Knowles, perhaps the son of the founder of the firm. Born at Clifton, in 1881 he was aged fifty-one, and lived at High Bank, North Road, Pendlebury with his wife Eleanor and their five daughters and one son, Robert who was a colliery manager. Another branch of the family, perhaps the most famed, was Sir James Lees Knowles, Bart (1857–1928). He was to preside over the coal mines at Agecroft, Little Lever, Clifton Hall and Pendlebury, employing in total over 3,400 men during the 1880s, producing over one million tons per annum, or twenty per cent of the output of all Lancashire pits. James Lees Knowles was elected as Conservative Member of Parliament for West Salford and was a keen athlete in his younger days. His father, John, was already a notable industrialist and influential local entrepreneur who also owned a cotton spinning factory, and was the first Chairman of the Swinton and Pendlebury Local Board. He was also a Justice of the Peace, an Alderman to Lancashire County Council and Deputy Sheriff of Lancashire. On the death of his father in 1894, James Lees inherited the chairmanship of the firm Andrew Knowles and Sons along with many large properties and estates in and around Pendleton.

James went on to own and live at Turton Tower near Bolton where many of his ancestors were buried. Like his father and uncles before him, he was bitterly opposed to any of the mining reforms brought in to improve the miners' lot, including trade unionism, the Eight Hours Act and the Working Men's Compensation Scheme. 'These' he said, 'would have made my work more difficult'. By the time of 1926 general strike the formerly great mining company of Andrew Knowles and Sons had ceased to exist. On his death two years later, 7 October 1928, his personal fortune was estimated to be around £227,000.

The first reports of the Clifton Hall Colliery Disaster came from local newspapers, in particular the *Manchester Guardian*. However, in their haste to get out the information there were many discrepancies. In view of this I have chosen to take the extracts of the report of the disaster from the Report of the Mine Inspectors for the year 1885, compiled by Joseph Dickinson, the senior inspector for the area. Firstly, Dickinson provides us with useful background detail about the colliery:

THE CLIFTON HALL COLLIERY, in which the great explosion of fire-damp took place on the 18th June 1885, whereby 178 lives were lost, is situated in the township of Clifton, about 4½ miles from Manchester, and within a ½ mile of Clifton Junction, on the Lancashire and Yorkshire Railway. There are two shafts, which were commenced about 50 years ago, and by which during about 30 years the Rams and other upper seams or mines were worked, until the shafts were sunk to the present mines. The depth now to the Cannel Mine is 595 yards, but that seam is only sunk to and not, yet worked, the depth to the present hooking-on place, which is at the Trencherbone Mine, being 534 yards, from which point the Trencherbone and overlying Five Quarters and Doe Mines are being worked. The lower part of the shafts, where there are no

The Clifton Hall Colliery a few years prior to the great explosion of 1885. From a picture postcard.
Peter Nadin collection

workings, serves as standage room for water, and is full of water nearly up to the Trencherbone Mine. The shafts are 10 yards apart. The winding shaft, which is the downcast for air, is 10 feet diameter, and is fitted with wooden conductors and two cages. The other shaft, which is upcast for air, is 9 feet in diameter, and is without internal fittings, but there is a capstan engine with pulleys and rope ready for use in either of the shafts when required. In addition to these two shafts there is a travelling way between this colliery and the Agecroft Colliery, where there are two windings shafts, which belong to the same owners, this communication was not made or used for working the coal, but only for an occasional travelling way, such as when repairs were being made in connection with the shafts or engines at either of the collieries, and the two collieries are kept distinct by means of four separation doors. The hooking-on place at Clifton Hall is in solid rock, a little above the Trencherbone coal, and about it are spacious chambers for manoeuvring the coal tubs, and for steam boilers, engines, offices, stables, &c., lighted with gas brought from above ground.

The level course runs nearly true east and west, and the strata dip southwards at the rate of about 1 in 3½. From the south side of the winding shaft a spacious level tunnel or stone drift, worked by engine and an endless chain, crosses through the dipping strata until the overlying Five Quarters and the Doe Mine is each intersected. And at the east side of the shaft there is in Trencherbone Mine an engine brow or incline to the dip, where the lower workings are 700 yards beneath the surface. The portion of all the seams on the rise of the shafts had been worked out some years ago, leaving only a large pillar in each seam for the support of the shafts. There is also a continuous pillar left in all the seams against the Great Irwell Valley fault, which throws the strata down 1,000 yards at the opposite side. The Doe Mine, or, as it is occasionally called, the Dow

Mine, is the uppermost seam of the three which are now being worked. It was sunk through in the shafts at 422 yards. The seam is 9 feet 4 inches in thickness, of which about 72 feet is good coal. The present workings are on the rise of levels driven from the end of the tunnel. Those in the east level have nearly worked back to the tunnel, but those on the west side are out about 1 to ¾ mile. The Five Quarters Mine lies 14 yards below the Doe, it is a thin seam and is worked by short tunnels driven from the Doe workings. The Trencherbone Mine, in which the explosion took place, lies 98 yards below the Five Quarters. It is here a clean bed of fine splint coal, about 6 feet in thickness, with a roof of about 2 yards of hard white sandy shale, called white metal-stone, including about a foot of worthless coal, called the California or Cally, and above that is 21 yards of solid rock, known as the Trencherbone Rock.

Mr Dickinson then described the day of the explosion, and his involvement:

Work was going on as usual at 20 minutes past 9 o'clock in the morning of the 18th June 1885 when a loud report, with smoke and dust, issued from the shafts. This continued for a few seconds, some flame coming out of the downcast. The current then reversed in the ordinary upcast and became downcast, which continued minutes, the smoke for 13 minutes being black and the remaining 2 minutes white, a which the currents in both shafts reversed into the natural course. Information of the occurrence was communicated to me by special messenger, whereupon I telegraphed to Mr. Martin, the inspector of mines, who has assisted many years in the district, and to

The scene at Clifton Hall Colliery on the day of the disaster, as illustrated in the local newspaper.
Author's collection

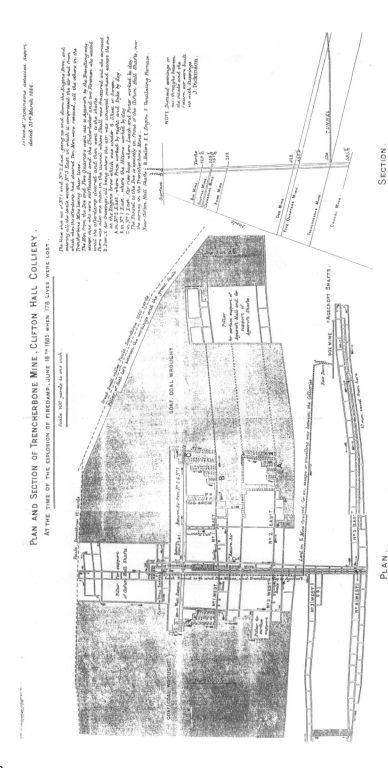

Plan of the workings of the Trencherbone Mine at Clifton Hall Colliery, taken from the mines inspector's report. Author's collection

Mr. Turton, the newly appointed assistant inspector. I arrived at the colliery about 11 am, and was followed at about 3 pm by Mr. Martin, and in the evening by Mr. Turton, both of them being at other collieries when my message arrived. On my way to the colliery I found men from it were coming out by Agecroft Colliery some of whom were suffering apparently from the effects of after-damp and over-exertion in escaping by the travelling way from Clifton Hall Colliery; and on arriving at Clifton Hall Colliery I found the winding cages fast in the downcast shaft, and the manager, with Aaron Manley, pit carpenter, and George Hindley, blacksmith, at work, using the capstan and hoppet to loosen them. The cages it appeared had been nearly at meetings when the explosion took place, running at full speed, when both cages received the force of the blast and were sustained by the safety catches, with loose rope dangling.

The manager having come up, giving his place to Peter Horsefield, I conferred with him and with Mr. Simon Horrocks the agent, as to the best mode of procedure, and subsequently I took part in the explorations, going into the mine on six occasions, Mr. Martin assisting throughout, and Mr. Turton occasionally. At 12 o'clock noon the cages were loosened, and the shaft repaired sufficiently to admit being used, when the manager and Mr. Horrocks, with Mr. Israel Barker and Mr. Wallwork managers from other collieries belonging to the same owners, accompanied by Aaron Manley pit-carpenter, and Robert Ogden, descended in the first cage.

It has not been by any means so usual as it deserves to mention the names of the principal explorers, there being seldom, if ever, any lack of heroic devotion, even on less stirring occasions when scarcely any except the few helpers know what has to be done, and they themselves do not consider it extraordinary, but as on this occasion some of the principal ones have been selected for decoration, I have added my tribute by here recording them. They were found amid the destruction at the bottom that Thomas Worrall, the underlooker of the Doe and the Five, Quarters Mine, and two of his firemen, Charles Parkinson and George Higson, had arrived there first. They, it appeared having been in the Doe Mine near the end of the tunnel when the explosion happened, and having first, together with a metal-stone man, who helped, fetched the men from the extreme far ends of the workings, and directed them out by the travelling way to Agecroft, and then when the after-damp was partially cleared made their way along the tunnel to the Clifton Hall shafts.

The rescuers also found that Mr. John Crook, manager of Agecroft Colliery, and one of his underlookers, Thomas Williams, had arrived there soon after Worrall, Crook with a party of men having gone in by the travelling way from Agecroft but, meeting sufferers on the way, all his party except himself and the underlooker, had to return and help them out. It also appeared that Crook and Worrall, having done what they could amongst the dead and dying, put out what fire was left at the ventilating furnace and the steam boiler. It was then quite apparent that a terrible explosion had taken place in the Trencherbone Mine. The survivors from about the bottom of the shafts were speedily sent out, all of them, except one, with his skull fractured and, being so seriously injured died; this man, along with ten others who were afterwards rescued from the extreme far end, were all that survived, except for those from the Doe and Five Quarters Mines. Arrangements having been made, the workings were forthwith penetrated so far as falls and afterdamp allowed. The part about the shafts and in the engine-brow, having a rock roof, was left almost intact, but No. 1 East Level from the engine-brow was found fallen, and the rock above was grinding as though it had been shaken or a ground weight had occurred, and No. 2 East was inaccessible on account of afterdamp; as was the engine-brow further down. Exploration continued. Air-doors, air-crossings or overcasts and the furnace were found blown away, tubs and other loose things were lying about shattered, the steam pipe from the boilers to the engines blown upbrow from where it crossed the engine brow. In the levels and workings props and chocks were blown out and the stone between the coal and the rock fallen, whilst the men seemed to have been struck dead, some at work and some at breakfast. A large body of gas must have been ignited, more than would be emitted from one or two places, and the flame had extended through most of the workings. The main blast had come out of No. 1 and No. 2 East, and in the engine-brow it divided, part going up brow to the shafts and part going down and entering the other levels at both sides. Way was made past falls. Temporary screens of tarpaulin were put in to replace some of the doors and crossings. Stretchers made of two poles with a tarpaulin between, were used for carrying the bodies over the falls. Firedamp was found in the extreme rise working in No. 1 and in No. 2 East. Some burning fire was found under a fall at the West Side. The critical operations requisite were all effected expeditiously and safely, and with the usual nobleness of character, which characterises miners on such occasions.

Whilst the exploration was progressing, and before it was known whether any part of the mine had been set on fire and remained burning, the ventilation suddenly reversed, which drove the explorers out by the travelling way to Agecroft. Brickwork, loosened by the blast, had fallen in the upcast shaft and reversed the air. The fall of the brickwork also opened an old cut-through between the two shafts, via which the emerging afterdamp passed from the upcast shaft and fouled the air in the downcast. This opening was temporarily stopped with bags of hay and sawdust, which served the purpose of keeping the afterdamp in the upcast and allowing the explorations to be continued until it was safe to light the ventilating fires, when the bags were taken out and new brickwork put in, which occasioned a short delay.

The rescue of ten men from the extreme far end of the Trencherbone Mine, under such circumstances, may be considered miraculous and shows that, under even the most discouraging appearances, hope should be sustained and efforts continued, until facts are ascertained. These men were in No. 3 East, which consisted of three levels from the bottom of the engine-brow, but which were not cut through to the level above, so that the flame and blast could not sweep round this part as it did in all the other levels, but merely compressed, the air in both the intake and the return. One of these men, Samuel Travis, described how pressure of air blew out all their candles and all the safety lamps which they had for testing with, except two; and that when they tried to escape they were stopped by afterdamp, and had to return. They tried again, with the same result at 2 o'clock but at 4.30 six of the men were able to enter the engine-brow, and reach the shaft at 10 o'clock at night. The four others were helped out afterwards. The horse that was with them died from suffocation or exhaustion.

The inquest

The main inquest was held by Mr. Frederick Price, county coroner, at the Pendlebury Institute and concerned 177 bodies. A secondary inquest related to one body, found afterwards under one of the numerous large falls of roof. Evidence was taken in the case of each body and every one was identified, thus avoiding the mistakes and anxieties which might otherwise have arisen.

At the opening of the main inquest, on 17 November 1884, Mr. Dickinson informed the coroner that he had received an undated anonymous letter with respect to the state of the Trencherbone Mine, and that consequently, next morning, Mr. Martin had made an inspection and inquiry. Giving evidence, Mr. Martin stated that on the occasion referred to he found that previous to his visit there was gas in Joseph Derricott's bay in

No. 2 East, where an airway became stopped, and that the men were sent home. He saw Derricott who explained that he had released the air right up to No. 1 level, and he (Mr. Martin) went to the face on the East and the West Side levels, and on No. 3 level, and through the bays and airways on No. 2 East, where he found naked lights in use in all places; and although he tried for gas a long way in the goaves (wastes), he neither found nor heard of any having been discovered recently except in Derricott's bay, where the new airway had been made.

Betsy Taylor, widow of Thomas Taylor, one of the ventilating furnace tenters, stated that her husband told her an explosion would occur, and repeated this comment the night before it occurred. Thomas said that the airways were not now so that a person could walk in straight up as it used to be when the late Mr. John Barker was manager, 3½ years ago; also that at Christmas 1883, when Clifton Hall shafts were being repaired and he had to go through the travelling way to Agecroft, the way was so low that he had to go almost on his hands and knees, and he was thankful to get back again. The air was so bad as to require the furnace to be kept fired up on Sundays. He also complained of the slack or small coal which he had to burn, being so bad that he could not loosen the clinkers from the furnace. She was not aware that he had ever made any complaint or representation to the mine managers, the underlookers or firemen. Had he done so, he might have lost his situation. Her son (deceased) also complained to her in Whit-week, and repeated it three days before the explosion, that the roof was loose and dangerous where he worked.

Thomas Wallwork, a friend of the deceased furnace tenter, confirmed what the widow stated, adding that better coal was given to burn, when the inspector was expected.

Ellen Hilton, widow of William Hilton, who had worked twenty-six years for the owners, of which the last two years were as a collier at Clifton Hall, ten years at Pendleton where for a period he acted as a fireman and, the previous time in Clifton Hall Colliery, stated that for a long time her husband told her an explosion would happen at that the place, that he and his brothers worked in a safe place, but there was fouling in other places and they (the men) were not aware of it.

Ann Hilton, widow of Thomas Hilton, who was a brother of William Hilton, and who had also been a fireman at Pendleton Colliery until a year or two ago, when they came as colliers to Clifton Hall, stated that the places were not looked after as they ought to be, there was carelessness and that at Christmas she heard William say something would happen. The two brothers left Pendleton Colliery shortly after their father ceased being an underlooker there.

Harriet Ann Hilton, widow of John Hilton, a coal-miner and brother of William and Thomas Hilton, stated that the three Hiltons said they never knew such carelessness as there was amongst the underlookers; there was a deal of gas either in their place or in the mine. William told her and her sisters-in-law many times since Christmas there would be an explosion, and he and his brothers would be brought home dead; that a while since the underlooker wanted them to go into a place which was full of gas, but they would not go because it was not fit to work in; he would not allow them enough wagons when they had plenty of coal to send out. She told her husband it was his duty to tell the underlooker or the fireman, to which he did not reply; that he was for weeks without seeing the underlooker that he did not complain to any one; that Mr. Dickinson, the inspector, did not seem to come, and Mr. William Pickard, the miners' representative of the district, was never mentioned; that the three brothers were all good scholars; they kept their complaints in the family; they used candles in the mine but never spoke of that practice as being dangerous.

John Tatlock, a retired miner, who until three years ago had worked in the Trencherbone Mine since it was started in May 1865, stated that up to his time it was as good and as well a fitted-up place as he ever worked at in his life; fire-damp appeared at times, and it came generally from the goaf; that his son John, deceased, told him six weeks before the explosion that he had heard there would be a fire before long, and he had asked the underlooker to allow him to shift to another mine, but he would not; that his place, which was on the west side and a very bad one – not for gas, but because there was plenty of coal and he could not get wagons enough to take it away, and that prevented his making enough wages.

Sarah Jackson, widow of Shimei Jackson, coal miner in the Doe Mine, and who was one of those who lost his life in the travelling way to Agecroft, stated that he told her the night before the explosion there was a very bad return of air in the Doe Mine, and there would be an explosion if something was not altered.

George Battersby, coal miner on No. 1 East level, stated that the Hiltons' bay was up in the workings, and his next to it, nearer the level. He did not hear an explosion until after it had occurred. A young man named Johnson told him since, and Hilton's wife told him.

William Buck, a night-fireman, stated that he fell ill on the last Saturday before Whit-week (23rd May) and that all gas met with was reported in his book, including that in Robins' and Derricott's bay, No. 2 East, on 22 October 1884, when coal had fallen in the airway; that a good airway was afterwards made, and that before the explosion happened that bay and another one further out were finished. He did not find any gas for three months before he left; the workings were in a fair state, and no gas coming out of the old workings. No workman ever complained to him, neither did he hear any rumour of danger before the explosion, nor had he any foreboding. (NB. The night fireman's book with the entry for 22 October 1884 was produced, but the succeeding one, terminating before Whit-week, was said to be 'lost'. There was no night-work in Whit-week. The night-fireman's book, commencing with the work after Whit-week, when a new fireman began, was produced.)

Thomas Buckley stated that for three years he had been employed as a day wageman in the mine, chiefly in No. 1 and No. 2 East districts. The airways were good all the time, and he never saw them in a bad condition. He was in the airway from No. 1 East a fortnight or three weeks since. It was 4 or 5 feet wide, and high enough for a man to walk straight up, and in the part where the East and West air travelled together it was 8 or 9 feet wide and 6 or 7 feet high. Falls (of roof) which took place were not stowed in airways, but put into the old waste. William Buck, the night fireman, having fallen ill, so this witness, when work was resumed on the 2 June, was appointed night-fireman, and acted as such until the 9th, when a successor was appointed. His reports were entered in a report book but, not being a scholar, they were written by the underlooker and he put his mark to them. The usual entry was the word 'Safe'. There were certain entries in the book made by William Buck which he inquired about, and he was told by the underlooker that they meant a bit of gas; and two or three of his own entries the underlooker said related to gas. These entries attracted his attention by being on the page opposite to that where 'Safe' was entered. He visited the furnace man twice every night. The furnace was cleaned twice every night. He never saw a bad fire. The furnace-man did not complain about the coal. Having resumed his day work, he was setting new timber in the pony shunt in No. 1 East during the night before the explosion. He began at 6.00 pm on the Wednesday and left at 5.40 next morning. The air was good, and the night fireman when on his round came to see him twice that night. He never heard any rumour of danger and was surprised to hear of the explosion. If there had been anything particular to put him in fear he would not have gone near the place.

Benjamin Crook, night-fireman, who commenced on 9 June after the temporary interval during which Thomas Buckley acted when William Ruck fell ill, stated that he was on duty during the night before the explosion. He did not find any gas that night, and the mine was all right when he left at quarter to six on the morning of the explosion. During the night, between 10.30 and 11.00, he was in No. 1 and No. 2 East, and did not perceive any 'weighting'. He had travelled the airway from No. 1 East to the furnace, and it was in a good state; but he had not travelled the airway from No. 2 to No. 1. The only gas which he found during his term as night-fireman was on 10 June (the explosion being on the 18th). It was a small quantity in Thomas Robins' bay, which is the second bay from the far end in No. 2 East. He entered a report of the gas in a book commencing with his term, which he produced.

George Battersby, coal miner, stated that he went to his work in No. 1 East at 4.30 pm the afternoon before, and left at 2.20 on the morning of the explosion. His place was a new bay 3 or 4 yards up from the level, and there were three or four bays beyond further up than his. The air was good, and the current so strong that candles which should have lasted two hours lasted only about forty minutes. He did not notice anything likely to lead to an explosion. The roof was solid enough and there was not any weighting. The night fireman came round twice that night. He worked previously 80 yards upbrow in a bay further in.

Samuel Travis, coal miner, stated that he was at Work in No. 3 East when the explosion happened, and was one of the ten men who came out alive and survived. John Colley, the fireman, was there when they began work at 6 in the morning and gave them an open light. He did not see any gas. A horse that was with them died from after-damp after the explosion.

Jonathan Hall, the certificated manager, stated that in the discharge of his duties he went down the pit at different times, sometimes before 6 in the morning, but generally about 9, and he conferred with the underlookers for about half-an-hour every afternoon between 3 and 4 o'clock. There was not any stint whatever by his employers in doing anything he wished or recommended being done for safety. He applied first to Mr. Horrocks the agent. The system of getting the coal was laid out on the plan, and then the sole charge was left to him. The ventilation was double what was required, and he always tried to regulate the currents so as not to travel too quickly. Doors, if left open, would take a portion of air from the workings. A fall in the airway between No. 2 and No. 1 East would slacken the air there. If this did not occur there had been a subsidence of roof behind No. 2. The airway from No. 2 was found fallen when he first saw it after the explosion, and it had apparently fallen at the time of the explosion; the fireman would go up there, and Price states that it had not fallen when he left on the morning of the explosion; the firemen's report books showed that ordinarily each fireman examined his return airways once a week and found them right, but in Thomas Hall's book, which referred to this part, the latest entry as to this airway from No. 2 to No. 1 East was on 5 June, or thirteen days before the explosion, which would occur either from his not being able to pass through, or from his omitting to enter it in his book. He did not think the ventilating furnace was being cleaned at the time of the explosion; it was cleaned twice at night and never by day.

He never saw any indication of gas coming to the furnace. He thought the explosion commenced in the far end place in No. 2 East, where Dyke works by day and Price at night, and that the gas came from the old goaf beyond; apparently the pillar of coal left for the support of Agecroft Hall supported the rock until the rock took a general weighting from that point, and produced a sudden outburst of gas; it appeared to have been sudden because the men were found, some with their picks and shovels in their hands, just as they were working. The explosion was a surprise to him, and the various colliers and night workmen on being informed of it, one and all, expressed their surprise. He never heard any rumour of danger, nor complaints about bad return of air, nor of the quality of the coal for the ventilating furnace, nor about the furnace having to be worked on Sundays, that having been commenced on Mr. Martin's recommendation, nor about the condition of the roof of the main roadways, except when Price complained, and that was rectified, and on the occasion of Mr. Dickinson the inspector's intimation, on 27 May last (which referred to the Doe Mine), when the underlookers and firemen were warned. There was no truth that different coal was supplied to the furnace when the inspectors were coming; he did not know when they were coming unless it was for a special reason. Mr. Dickinson, the inspector's name with his address was posted up on the Official Abstract of the Act and the special rules, in a conspicuous place. Mr. Dickinson was in the mine several times, and Mr. Martin, the assistant inspector, had been down two or three times this year, and Mr. Turton, the new assistant, once. Mr. Martin was there oftener than he liked.

Mr. Frederick Price, solicitor, who held the inquest, in summing up the main inquiry, said he had been sixteen years the coroner and thirteen years previously the deputy-coroner for the district, and he had frequently remarked how few fatal colliery accidents had lately occurred as compared with what occurred in the early part of his coronership, there having been only one explosion, and that from a blown-out shot, where more than one person had died from an explosion. The complaints given by witnesses as to conversations at home were very indefinite; it seemed incredible that men should go to work believing that at any moment a large quantity of gas might be emitted, and that the casualty which has happened could possibly happen in their mine. There was a singular unanimity of opinion expressed by the firemen and miners with respect to the general absence of a large amount of inflammable gas, and an equal unanimity with reference to the reliance that is to be placed on the use of naked lights. Where there is a diversity of opinion, such as has been pressed by Mr. Dickinson upon the management for twenty-five years with respect to the use of naked lights, it seems somewhat out of place for the jury, who are not so skilled in these matters as they are, to express an opinion upon it, for supposing the jury did express an opinion, and in consequence of that opinion naked lights were discontinued and safety lamps used, and something should happen which might be put down to the change, it would be said at once this was done at the request of the jury, and the same with regard to the kind of lamp that should be substituted.

The jury on 9 July returned a verdict to the effect that the deaths were 'accidental'; that the explosion was of firedamp suddenly and unexpectedly emitted from goaves or old workings, and was ignited at a candle; that seeing the diversity of opinion which has existed as to the use of naked lights, the jury declined to express any opinion, but recommended that it be referred for consideration, and that in their opinion Mr. Dickinson was justified in withholding from the knowledge of the managing director of the colliery the contents of the anonymous letter in November 1884, referred to in his and Mr. Martin's evidence.

Another body having been found under a large fall, making 178 deaths, a further inquest was held by Mr. Price on 27 July, with a new jury, but including some members of the former one. It was stated by Mr. Hall, the manager, that since the explosion he had received 500 applications for work in the Trencherbone Mine; safety lamps had been introduced exclusively; but many of the men would prefer to work with candles, especially the old workmen; they prefer candles because they can see so much better; they think there will be more fatalities from falls of ground with using lamps. The further explorations confirmed him in the opinion that the gas came out of the goaf consequent upon a weight taking place and not from any interruption in the airway. On this occasion the coroner put it to the jury whether in their opinion candles or safety lamps should be used; eleven were in favour of using lamps and three in favour of candles.

As in all mining disasters there were many brave acts during the rescue attempts, and in the case of the Clifton Hall Colliery disaster some of the rescue workers were rewarded with the Albert Medal, as reported below:

INVESTITURE. Her Majesty the Queen, on the recommendation of Sir Richard Assheton Cross, Secretary of State, was graciously pleased to confer 'The Albert Medal of the First Class' upon Mr. Thomas Worrall, underlooker of the Doe and Five Quarters Mine, Clifton Hall Colliery, and upon Mr. John Crook, manager of the Agecroft Colliery. The Queen, on the same recommendation, was also graciously pleased to confer 'The Albert Medal of the Second Class' upon Mr. Charles Parkinson, fireman, Doe and Five Quarters Mine, Clifton Hall Colliery; Mr. George Higson, fireman, Doe and Five Quarters Mine, Clifton Hall Colliery; Mr. Aaron Manley, pit carpenter, Clifton Hall Colliery; Mr. George Hindley, blacksmith, Clifton Hall Colliery.

The ceremony took place at the Institute, Pendlebury, on Friday evening, 6 November 1885, when there was a large attendance. It was intended that the universally respected Bishop of Manchester (Dr Fraser), with the Mayor of Manchester, both of whom were at the colliery during part of the explorations, should have jointly made the presentations, but the lamented death of the Bishop caused the whole to devolve upon the mayor. Mr Talbot, Deputy Town Clerk of Manchester, read a letter dated 5 October from the Secretary of State to the Mayor, asking him to present the decorations publicly. He also read a letter from the Bishop of Manchester, written during his illness. The Mayor in a touching address expressed the honour, which he felt in being called upon to present the Albert Medals, and his pleasure in seeing so many persons who had come to express their appreciation of the gallantry and heroism of the men who had to receive these medals.

All the above men received in addition to those medals, the Salford Humane Society Medal, and a further fifty-three men received illuminated addresses which were presented to those involved in the disaster, justification, were it needed, for the bravery of the many who took part.

Naked lights (candles) were never again used at the pits belonging to Andrew Knowles and Sons following this explosion. The year after the disaster, a ventilation fan was installed to replace the outdated furnace ventilation system. Time was running out though for the Clifton Hall Colliery, and the pit was abandoned forever in 1933 when worked by the Manchester Collieries Ltd. It continued to claim lives almost to the very end for, in January 1930, John Devonport was killed through being trapped between the cage and some machinery. At the time of the abandonment, Clifton Hall Colliery employed 572 underground workers and 287 surface men. There is no evidence today of the Clifton Hall Colliery where so great a loss of life occurred all those years ago, no great memorial stands on the site to tell newer generations of this tragic explosion. All is now silent.

Those who perished at Clifton Hall Colliery were:

Aston, William aged 52, coal miner, 17 Moore Street, widower, with 2 children
Allen, John aged 29, hooker-on, 22 Back Oak Street, Pendlebury, married*
(The grave of John Allen can be seen at the Parish Church, Pendlebury)
Atkinson Israel, aged 22, coal miner, 126 Bolton Road, Pendlebury, single
Atkinson John aged 40 coal miner, 60 New Street Pendlebury, married, 6 children
Banks Reuben aged 19, jigger, 9 Worsley Street, Newton, single
Barker, Walter aged 16, stable boy, single of 12 Carrington Street*
Barlow Frederick aged 23, coal miner, 20 Carrington Street, Pendlebury, single
Barlow Noah aged 20, coal miner, 20 Carrington Street, Pendlebury, single
Barlow Thomas (jnr) aged 22, coal miner, 23 Long Street, Swinton, married, 1 child
Barlow Thomas aged 54, coal miner, 20 Carrington Street, Pendlebury, married,
    6 children
Barter Leonard Charles, aged 13, waggoner of 9 Oldham Street, Pendlebury, single
Baxter William aged 20, coal miner of 20 Spencer Street, single**
Bell Benjamin aged 18, coal miner of 32 New Street, single
Berry George Enoch aged 20, waggoner of Albion Street, Pendlebury, single**
Berry John aged 16, a jigger, 66 Bolton Road, Clifton, single
Berry William aged 54, coal miner, Albion Street, Pendlebury, married**
Blomerby James aged 47, coal miner, Bank Lane, Pendlebury, married, 3 children
Blower Walter aged 28, coal miner, Victoria Terrace, married, 1 child
Booth William aged 17, waggoner, Harrol Gate, single
Bradley Thomas (senr) aged 43, coal miner, 4 George Street, widower, with 4 children
Bradley William aged 20, pony driver, 30 City Walk, Pendlebury, single
Brooks Matthew aged 16, waggoner, 15 Algernon Street, Swinton, single
Buck Thomas Percival, aged 18, waggoner, Partington Lane Swinton, single
Cheadle Richard aged 24, coal miner, Dowing Street, Swinton, single
Clamp Joseph aged 44, coal miner, 8 Bridge Street, Pendlebury, married, 6 children
Colley John, aged 37, fireman, 9 Oak Street, Pendlebury, married, 4 children
Colley Joseph aged 35, coal miner, 81 Clifton Terrace, married, 3 children
Collier John aged 35, bricklayer, 5 Folly Lane Swinton, married, no children
Collier Thomas aged 19, taker-off, 7 Melbourne Street, Pendlebury, single
Constine John, aged 33, stoker, Algernon Street, Pendlebury, married, 3 children
Crook James aged 23, foreman, 96 Bolton Road, Pendleton, married*
Crook James aged 40, coal miner, 56 Jane Lane Swinton, married with 11 children
Crook John aged 19, coal miner, 103 Jane Lane, Swinton, single**
Crook Ralph aged 44, coal miner, 103 Jane Lane, Swinton, married, 8 children**
Crossley Robert aged 32, coal miner, 70 Harrol Gate, Swinton, single
Daniels Ralph, aged 65, labourer, 46 Granville Street, Swinton, married, 4 children
Darby William aged 23, filler, 60 Jane Lane, Swinton, single
Davies David, aged 20, coal miner, 4 City Walk, Pendlebury, single
Davies Edward, aged 36, coal miner, 3 John Street, Jane Lane, married, 3 children
Davies John (junior) aged 15, waggoner, 4 City Walk, single
Davies John (senior) aged 56, coal miner, 4 City Walk, married 2 children
Davies John aged 26, coal miner of 26 Oak Street, Pendlebury, married, 1 child
Davies Joseph aged 26, coal miner, 32 New Street, Pendlebury, married, 3 children
Dermody John aged 20, wagon filler, 74 Harrol Gate, single

Derricott Joseph aged 39, coal miner, Harrol Gate Swinton, married, 4 children
Done John aged 34, coal miner, 3 Jackson's Buildings, married, 3 children
Doxey David, aged 43 underlooker, 311 Bolton Road, Pendlebury, married with
  3 children.
Dunkerley John Henry, aged 19, waggoner, Brindle Heath, Pendleton, single
Dunn Thomas aged 26, coal miner, 13 Cotton Street, Clifton, widower
Dyke John aged 31, coal miner, Muske Buildings, Swinton, married
Dyson James aged 33, coal miner, 43 Grosvenor Street, Pendlebury, married, 3 children
Dyson Joseph aged 24, coal miner, 4 City Walk, Pendlebury, married, 2 children
Dyson Samuel, aged 24, coal miner, Rake Lane Swinton, married, 2 children
Eaves Samuel aged 27, daywageman, Cavendish Street, Pendlebury, married, 1 child

The grave of John Allen who lost his life at Clifton Hall Colliery can be seen at the parish church, Pendlebury. The author

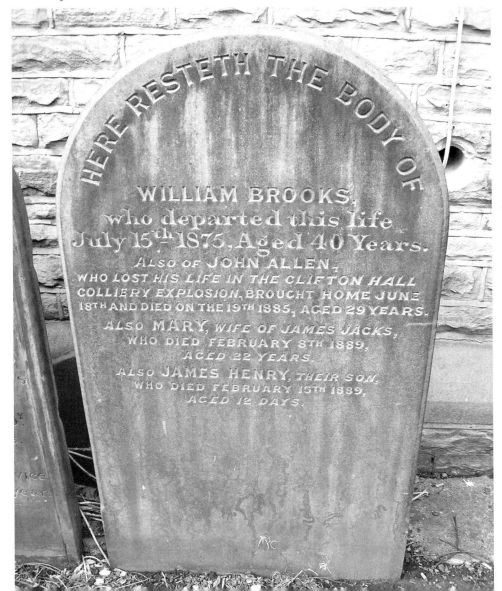

Eckersley John aged 33, coal miner, 18 Hilton Street, Pendlebury, single
Edge Ernest aged 18, coal miner, 75 New Street, Pendlebury, single
Edwards John aged 29, coal miner, 8 Holland Street Swinton, married
Edwards Thomas aged 27, coal miner, 30 Jane Lane Swinton, married, no children
Edwards William Henry aged 20, coal miner, Banks Buildings, single
Evans John aged 25, engine driver, Rake Lane, Clifton married no children
Ewing Walter aged 20, coal miner, 5 Park Street, Swinton, single
Feeney James aged 21, coal miner, 8 Redmond Street, Pendlebury, single
Franklin William aged 23, waggoner, 5 Richmond Street, Clifton, single
Gardner Luke age 29, coal miner, 132 Bolton Road, Pendlebury, single
Gaskell Charles Edward aged 20, coal miner, 4 Bolton Road, Clifton, single
Gee William aged 18, waggoner, 30 Union Street, single
Green Henry aged 28 coal miner, 98 Jane Lane, Swinton, married, 3 children
Greenhalgh Edwin aged 19, coal miner, 33 Union Street, single
Greenhalgh John William, aged 16, taker-off, 73 Jane Lane Swinton, single
Gretton John aged 17, waggoner, 11 Wellington Street, single
Griffiths Isaiah, aged 47, coal miner, Lings Buildings, Swindon, widower, with
    3 children
Grimshaw Herbert aged 15 waggoner, 48 Union Street, single
Hall George aged 42, daywageman, 9 Oldham Street, Pendlebury, married, 3 children
Hall Thomas, aged 42, fireman, 110 Prestwich View, Pendlebury, married with 1 child.
Hall William aged 25, daywageman, 432 Twenty Row, Pendlebury, married
Hardman Daniel, aged 37 ostler, 28 City Walk, Pendlebury, married, no children
Hardman John aged 25, hooker-on, 22 Back Oak Street Pendlebury, married, 1 child*
Hardman John, aged 24, coal miner, 108 Turton Row, Clifton, widower with 3 children
Hardman Thomas aged 28, hooker-on, 22 Back Oak Street, Pendlebury, married,
    5 children*
Hilton John, aged 26, coal miner, 5 Muirhead Street, married, 1 child
Hilton Thomas aged 29, coal miner, 4 Muirhead Street, married, 1 child
Hilton William aged 36, coal miner, 134 Whit Lane, Pendlebury, married, 2 children
Hopwood James aged 15, waggoner, 17 Burying Lane, Swinton, single
Hotchkins Thomas, aged 14, waggoner, 23 Thomas Street, single
Howell John aged 21, coal miner, 7 Moore Street, Pendlebury, single
Hughes James aged 20, waggoner, 15 Cobden Street, single
Hughes John aged 18, daywageman, 28 Spencer Street, Pendlebury, single
Humphreys Edward, aged 23, coal miner, 132 Bolton Road, Pendlebury, single
Jackson Sheinei, aged 39, coal miner, 39 Union Street, married**
Johnson Daniel aged 36, coal miner, Chalmer's Buildings, married, 4 children
Johnson William aged 32, coal miner, 4 Church Street, Irlam, single
Jones Enoch aged 29, coal miner, 23 Thomas Street, married, 4 children
Jones Samuel aged 24, taker off, 19 George Street, single*
Jones William aged 33, coal miner, 132 Bolton Road, Pendlebury, married, 1 child
Kay James aged 35, coal miner, 175 Jane Lane, Swinton, married, 5 children
Kilner Samuel, aged 14, furnace man's helper, 37 Downing Street Swinton, single
Kimer Peter, aged 30, wagon oiler, 37 Downing Street, single*
Leach Samuel, aged 37, coal miner, 54 Union Street, widower
Loader George, aged 22, coal miner, 44 Lonsdale Street, Swinton, single
Lycett William, aged 16, Franchise Street, single*
Madden George, aged 21, waggoner, 9 Birkdale Grove, single
Maddon George, aged 21, waggoner, 9 Birkdale Grove, Newtown, single

Mannion John, aged 23, coal miner, Holland Street, Swinton, married, 4 children
Marshall Harry, other details unknown
Matthews Samuel, aged 21, coal miner, Cobden Street, Pendlebury, single
Mattox Henry aged 23, coal miner, 1 Cobden Street, Pendlebury, married, 1 child
Mattox Thomas aged 24, coal miner, 22 Old Street, Clifton, married
Mawdsley William aged 16, waggoner, 23 Engine Brow, single
McCarthy John, aged 17, waggoner, 24 Saxby Street, Irlam, single
McHugh Patrick, aged 38, coal miner, 140 Bolton Road, Pendlebury, single
Mellins John, aged 16, waggoner, 8 Holland Street, Swinton, single
Merrick William Henry, aged 19, filler, 56 Oak Street, Pendlebury, single
Morris Thomas aged 40, coal miner, 66 New Street, Pendlebury, single
Page William, aged 37, coal miner, 33 Eaton Street, Worsley, married with 6 children
Parkinson William, aged 17, coal miner, 169 Jane Lane, Swinton, single
Parry Alfred, aged 31, daywageman, 15 Holland Street, single
Parry Thomas, aged 31, daywageman, 15 Holland Street, single
Pearson Joseph, aged 49, daywageman, 13 Park Street, Swinton, married, 5 children*
Penny Henry John, aged 29, daywageman, married, 1 child
Porter Daniel, aged 35, coal miner, 50 Union Street, Pendlebury, single
Porter Kay, aged 40, coal miner, 53 Union Street, married, 5 children
Porter Samuel, aged 14, waggoner, 53 Union Street, single
Price Joseph, aged 29, coal miner, 35 George Street, married, 5 children
Pugh James Edward, aged 20, coal miner, Harrol Gate Villas, Swinton, single
Quinnan John, aged 20, daywageman, 23 Worlsey's Buildings, single
Redford James, aged 21, coal miner, Spence Street, single
Reid William Henry, aged 16, filler, 73 Bury Lane Pendlebury, single
Reynolds William, aged 20, daywageman, 183 Jane Lane Swinton, single
Riley John (junior), aged 20, waggoner, 11 Bolton Road, single
Riley John (senior), aged 44, coal miner, 11 Bolton Road, Pendlebury, married,
    6 children
Riley William, aged 17, waggoner, 11 Bolton Road, single
Roberts Edward, aged 19, horse driver, 26 Torrens Street, Pendleton, single
Roberts George, aged 25, wagon filler, 30 New Street, Pendlebury, single**
Robins Thomas, aged 33, coal miner, 24 Saxby Street, Pendlebury, married, 6 children
Rothwell James, aged 23, coal miner, 20 The Deans, Swinton, married 1 child
Rushton William, aged 17, waggoner, 19 Birkdale Grove, Swinton, single
Ryder John, aged 46, coal miner of Bridge Street, Pendlebury, married, 3 children
Ryder William, aged 48, coal miner, 19 Grosvenor Street, Newtown, married with
    7 children
Sackfield John, aged 48, coal miner, 32 Union Street, married, 7 children
Sackfield Thomas, aged 13, waggoner, 32 Union Street, single
Seddon Richard, aged 41, collier, 9 Hilton Street, Pendlebury, married, no children
Seddon Thomas aged 37, coal miner, 2 Hilton Square, Pendlebury, married, 5 children
Sefield Edward, aged 20, coal miner, 5 Moore Street, Pendlebury, married, 1 child
Sharples Samuel, aged 34, coal miner, 56 Bolton Road, Clifton, married, 7 children
Slattery Thomas, aged 34, coal miner of 77 Jane Lane, married, 1 child
Smethills John, aged 32, coal miner, 23 Alice Street, Swinton, married, 6 children
Staley Thomas, aged 23, coal miner, Pott Street, Newtown, single
Staziker Alfred, aged 16, waggoner, 10 Bold Street, Newton, single
Sutton John, aged 20, waggoner,7 Melbourne Street, Pendlebury, married, 2 children
Tatlock James, aged 21, coal miner, 19 Old Street, Clifton, single

Taylor Hamlet, aged 30, coal miner, 9 Bury Lane, married, 5 children
Taylor John, aged 16, waggoner, Harrol Gate, Swinton, single
Taylor John Hamlet, aged 20, coal miner 91 Manchester Road, Worsley, single
Taylor John, aged 44, coal miner, 22 Carrington Street, single
Taylor Thomas, aged 44, furnace man, married, 7 children
Turner James, aged 34, fireman, Irlam-o'-th'-Heights, married, 3 children
Turner William, aged 30, daywageman, 23 Union Street, Pendlebury, married, 1 child
Valentine Albert, aged 27, bricklayer's labourer, Harrol Gate, Swinton, married, 7 children
Vickers James, aged 22, coal miner, 3 Thomas Street, Clifton, single
Vickers Samuel, aged 56, coal miner, Thomas Street, Pendlebury, married, 6 children
Wadsworth Ralph, aged 23, coal miner, Cavendish Street, Pendlebury, married 1 child
Wallace Arthur, aged 19, filler, 29 Union Street, single
Wardle William, aged 34, coal miner, 60 Bury Lane, Swinton, married, 4 children
Warren James, aged 17, waggoner of 42 New Street, Pendlebury, single
Whitehead Joseph, aged 30, coal miner, 19 Union Street, married, 2 children
Whittingham James, aged 34, hooker-on, 3 Hornby Street, married, 4 children*
Wilcox Peter, aged 17, filler, 8 Irlam Square, single
Williams James, aged 27, coal miner, 25 Torrens Street, married, 1 child
Williams Samuel, aged 16, pony driver, 22 Pitt Street, single
Williams Thomas, aged 19, daywageman, 63 Stapleton Street, single
Williams William, aged 30, coal miner, Cavendish Street, Pendlebury, single
Wolstenholme John, aged 25, coal miner, 6 Filton Street, Clifton, married, 1 child
Wolstenholme Peter, aged 25, coal miner, 15 Rake Lane, Clifton, married, 1 child
Worrall Robert, aged 13, waggoner, 12 Charles Street, Pendlebury, single**
Worsley Thomas, aged 28, wagon filler, 12 Kent Street, Pendleton, single**
Worthington George, aged 33, coal miner, 17 Cobden Street, Pendlebury, married, 4 children
Yates John, aged 20, coal miner, 6 Knowles Square, married, 3 children

Entries marked * were brought out of the pit alive, but died later; entries marked ** died in the Agecroft 'escape' tunnel. The above list is taken from the *official* record, but only shows 177 victims, of the supposed 178 who perished. The Clifton Hall Colliery Disaster made over 237 children orphans.

(32) Bedford Colliery, Leigh: 13 August 1886

Brown had his lamp hung from his belt by a strap when John Wolley noticed some gas inside Benjamin's lamp.

There is a large fine and fitting memorial to the colliery disaster of 1886 at Leigh cemetery which can be seen as you go through the entrance gates. The memorial is the large white structure topped with an urn at the top of the main drive, before the chapel. The colliery itself, also known as the Woodend Pit, was situated a few hundred yards back along Manchester Road at the top of Green Lane. The 'Woodend' in question being the Bedford or Hough Wood of Lilford Park to the west of the colliery. Coal mining in this area is reputed to have been in existence in the 1830s. On 21 December 1850 it was reported that William Clegg fell down an old pit shaft which was being filled at the Bedford Colliery and was killed. This Bedford pit was being worked by W E Milnes. However, by 1854 this pit, or one of

IN MEMORY OF
THOSE
WHO LOST THEIR LIVES IN
THE BEDFORD COLLIERY
EXPLOSION AUG: 13TH 1886.
BENJAMIN HILTON AGED 12
WILLIAM HEATON - 14
JOHN HILTON - 16
JOHN SIMS NUTTALL - 16
JOHN HENRY COOKE - 17
RICHARD BOWDEN - 28
HENRY SMITH - 58
THOMAS STIRRUP - 13
PETER STIRRUP - 18
WILLIAM STIRRUP - 43
JAMES BROWN - 46
THOMAS FAIRCLOUGH - 34
MICHAEL DANIELS - 44
ALLEN HADFIELD - 21
THOMAS HINDLEY - 41
HIRAM PEMBERTON - 38
ALLEN SHOVELTON - 25
PETER RADCLIFFE - 28

GENTLEMEN OF THE COMMITTEE.
WILLIAM HORNDEN   GERRARD JOHNSON
JAMES CALLAN   WILLIAM COLLIER
JOHN MEAKINS   JOHN HOLLAND

IN MEMORY OF
OUR DEAR COLLEAGUES

BEDFORD BRANCH

JAMES CALLAN   WILLIAM COLLIER
JOHN MEAKINS   JOHN HOLLAND

IN MEMORY OF
OUR DEAR COLLEAGUES
FROM MEMBERS OF
BEDFORD BRANCH N.U.M.
WHICH CLOSED FEB.24TH 1968.

(Above) The memorial to the victims of the Bedford Colliery Disaster, Leigh cemetery, and (Left) The National Union of Mineworkers' memorial to those who perished in the Bedford Colliery Disaster, Leigh cemetery. The author

this name, was worked by Samuel Jackson and Co. Around 1875 John Speakman commenced the sinking of the Nos. 1 and 2 Pits at the new Bedford Colliery to depths of 431 and 617 yards respectively; both these shafts had wooden headgear, and the sinking was completed in 1878. John Speakman died in 1873 but his name lived on in John Speakman and Sons. The original owner did not, therefore, live to see the greatest disaster to ever to befall the mine.

The two shafts at Bedford Colliery were about 30 yards apart, the No. 1 shaft being the upcast and 15 feet in diameter. The No. 2 shaft was downcast and 14 feet in diameter, but deepened to the Seven Feet or Black and White Seam in 1883. Water was a considerable problem during sinking, a feeder was met at 80 yards, and another one at 150 yards. To deal with this a lodgement was cut in the side of the upcast shaft and pumps were installed at that point.

The Seven Feet Mine was notoriously fiery, but the owners were aware of this and took every precaution, so only safety lamps were allowed underground. At the time of the disaster various levels in the mine extended a distance of 600 yards from the pit bottom. Around eleven o'clock on the morning of 13 August 1886, ironically a Friday, John Wolley was working in the furthest levels along with Benjamin Brown, filling a tub for a collier named Alfred Mort. Brown had his lamp hung from his belt by a strap when John Wolley noticed some gas inside Benjamin's lamp. Wolley shouted out a warning to Benjamin, who shook the lamp to try and get rid of the gas, but the gas burst through the gauze and was followed immediately by an explosion. John Wolley, who was about a yard away at the time, was thrown headlong and badly burned. He was well aware of what had happened and knew that he had to get out of the place before the afterdamp came, with its suffocating effects. In spite of his injuries, he picked himself up and began to run towards the shaft. Bodies lay in each and every direction and even then were beyond help. As Wolley approached the top of the last level he heard P Boardman, a fireman, crying out 'Jack, is it thee?'; and he replied 'Yes'. He informed Wolley that he had been down the last level, which Wolley was about to go, and told him that the afterdamp was too strong. 'There is nothing else for it', replied Wolley, 'it's life or death';and with that both men raced down the only way forward into the afterdamp, covering their faces with their caps. Incredibly, by climbing over roof falls, broken tubs and debris they got through and in the distance they saw a light, that of John Calland, the underlooker. The air was clearer now nearer the shaft bottom and the men pushed on although weakened, burnt and at the point of exhaustion. Remarkably, a number of other men had escaped from the seat of the explosion, but all the others, thirty-eight in number, had perished.

Those miners working on the other side of the shaft were unaware of the explosion, all they heard was a dull thud. It was only when the afterdamp came around to their workings did they realise what had happened. All these men were got safely out of the pit, and gave the alarm to the management. The explosion was not loud as far as pit disasters go, the only indication of the surface being a dark red-brown plume of smoke at the upcast shaft.

Exploring parties were formed immediately and, by six o'clock that night, had succeeded in reaching the far levels in spite of the thick afterdamp. The searchers

Bedford Colliery at Leigh, scene of the August 1886 disaster. From a picture postcard. Peter Nadin collection

had the experience of Joseph Dickinson, the Mines Inspector, who had arrived at the pit around three o'clock. The following day thirty-six bodies had been recovered from the workings, and a while later the last two men, William Brown and John Ward, were taken from the place they had died and removed to the pit top. All the dead men and boys were laid out in the joiners' shop and were identified without too much difficulty.

The inquest took place in the offices at the colliery before Mr J B Edge, coroner for the district. The first task was to make sure all had been identified, and then the bodies could be released, allowing the bereaved families to lay to rest their loved ones. Eighteen widows and fifty-four children were left to grieve following the explosion at the Bedford Colliery on that terrible day. Fortunately, all of the men and boys were members of the Lancashire and Cheshire Miners' Permanent Relief Society. The provision to be made by the Society was five shillings per week to each widow, and half a crown a week for each child until it was thirteen years of age. The saddest case was that of the Stirrup family, who lost a father and two sons; and many others were left to lament at their loss. In addition to these payments, an allowance was also made for funeral expenses. In the case of single men or boys, a payment of £20 was made or, if someone was dependent upon him, a weekly pension of five shillings per week granted.

Wolley was one of those who gave evidence. He stated that he had seen the gas explode at the safety lamp of the man filling the tub. No-one it appeared had ever seen the gas take fire at a Davy lamp, although previous explosions in other areas had been thought to have been caused through this. It was remarked that Wolley was probably the only man to have seen this occurance and lived through the subsequent explosion. His testimony would be of great value in the future. At last, the names of the dead men and boys could be named:

Benjamin Hilton, aged 18, Downcroft, Pennington

W. Heaton, aged 14, Coal Pit Lane, Bedford

John Hilton, aged 16, Trafalgar Street, Bedford

John Sims, aged 19, Millar Street, Bedford

Henry Smith aged 39, Marsh Street, Bedford, married to Mary with four children: Helen, George, William and Harry.

Richard Bowden aged 28, 95 Bradshaw Gate, Pennington, single, son of James, a beerseller, and Mary. He also left behind two brothers, James and Frederic.

Peter Stirrup, aged 18, 18, Dukinfield Street, Bedford.

Thomas Stirrup, aged 13, 18 Dukinfield Street, Bedford

William Stirrup, aged 43, 18 Dukinfield, Bedford, father of the above two, married with three children, the surviving child being a daughter named Mary.

James Brown, aged 46, Brewery Lane, Bedford, married with five children

Thomas Fairclough, aged 34, 66 Ellesmere Street, Pennington, married to Mary who was left with two children, John and Annie.

Michael Daniels, aged 44, 16 High Street, Bedford, married to Sarah, who was left with four children to bring up, Allan Radfield Daniels, Richard Daniels, and Maria Daniels.

Allen Hadfield Daniels, aged 21, 16, High Street Bedford, stepson of the above

Thomas Hindley aged 41, Spring View, Westleigh, married with two children

Hiram Pemberton, aged 38, Heatherstone Street, Pennington, married to Elizabeth, with five children, Elizabeth, Jane, John, Thomas and William.

Peter Ratcliffe, aged 25, the son of George and Ann, of Briggs Buildings, Westleigh, who also left a widow.

Allen Shovelton, aged 26, Abbey Street, Allerton, single

Thomas Hilton, aged 53, 7 Brown Street, Pennington, who left a widow, Mary Jane.

George Parkes, aged 24, Robinson Street, Bedford

Stephen Hampson, aged 55, Trafalgar Street, Bedford, who left a widow, Betsy.

Robert Hole, aged 65, Marsland Green, Astley, married with two children

William Eckersley, aged 54, Kirkhall Lane, Leigh

William Urmston, aged 17, Close Place, Bedford, the son of John a coal miner and Sarah.

Isaac Worthington, aged 40, Oxford Street, Allerton, married with three children

Thomas Killean, aged 17, Back Lane Westleigh

Michael Killean, aged 53, Back Lane, Westleigh, father of the above, married with five children

Thomas Smith, aged 18, Glebe Street, Westleigh

Thomas Smith, aged 52, Marsh Street, Bedford, father of the above

Robert Elliott, aged 17, Glebe Street, Westleigh

Henry Collier, aged 19, 22, Coal Pit Lane, Bedford, the son of Richard, coal miner and Margaret.

Joseph Hope, aged 44, Marsh Street, Bedford, left a widow and three children

Alfred Mort, aged 29, Dukinfield Street, Bedford, left a widow and two children, Betsy Ann and Margaret. Richard Mort, below was probably Alfred's brother; he was lodging with Richard a few years before the disaster.

Richard Mort, aged 26, Hampson Court, Bedford, left a widow and one child
Thomas Clayton, aged 25, Court, Walsh Hill, Bedford, left a widow and two children
Henry Parsonage, aged 41, Lord Street, Tyldesley, married with four children
William Brown, Sidney Street, Leigh
John Ward, aged 21, Albion Street, Leigh

John Ward was the final victim of the disaster recovered from the pit, though his features were unrecognisable. The poor fellow's mother had the terrible task of identifying her offspring, and settled the matter by the clothes he had worn that day. On Wednesday 17 August 1886, the bodies of eighteen of the men and boys who had perished in the disaster were interred at Leigh cemetery. The curtains were drawn the full length of the thoroughfares, and large grieving crowds viewed as silent witnesses. The funeral of William Brown was attended by the football team with which he was associated. Michael Killean (Killalee in some reports) was buried with his son in the same grave. It was all too much for his widow, who fainted at the graveside, and had to be removed. The others who had died at the pit were buried in the following days and the mothers, wives, sisters, brothers and fathers were then left on their own to mourn the sad losses.

The inquest returned the verdict of 'Accidental death' on all counts, casting doubts on the 'safety' of the Davy safety lamp in certain situations.

Bedford Colliery did recover from the events of that sad day in 1886, and a decade later was employing 366 underground workers and 108 surface workers. In March 1929 Bedford Colliery became part of the Manchester Collieries Ltd, and in December 1939 new pit-head baths were opened. On nationalisation of the British coal mining industry, 1 January 1947, Bedford Colliery Nos. 1 and 3 was mining coal from the White and Black, Five Quarters and Victoria Seams. Underground connections had been made with the Chanters Colliery at Atherton, and the system of ventilation was in common with both pits. Seven hundred and eight men were employed underground, together with further two 269 surface workers. Like all extraction industries, coal mining is dependant on its reserves of coal. By the mid-1960s reserves were running out at Bedford Colliery, coupled with the fact that some of the remaining coal was located under built-up areas. On February 24 1968 Bedford Colliery closed and over 700 men were thrown out of work. With the closure went the memories of the appalling events of August 1886, which then slipped silently away into the annals of coal mining history – but not before the local branch of the National Union of Mineworkers placed at monument to their dead comrades at the base of the memorial to the disaster at Leigh Cemetery. There are no remains whatsoever of the old Bedford Colliery, all has now been landscaped. The fine memorial to this disaster on the right-hand side of Leigh Cemetery, about 100 yards from the entrance gates, recalls the fateful day. The victims have not been forgotten.

(33) Bamfurlong Colliery, Bamfurlong, Wigan: 14 December 1892

The oil spread over the floor of the engine room, setting alight the wooden floor ...

Bamfurlong Colliery was situated off Lily Lane at Platt Bridge, about a quarter of a mile west of Bamfurlong Bridge over the Leeds and Liverpool Canal. Messrs

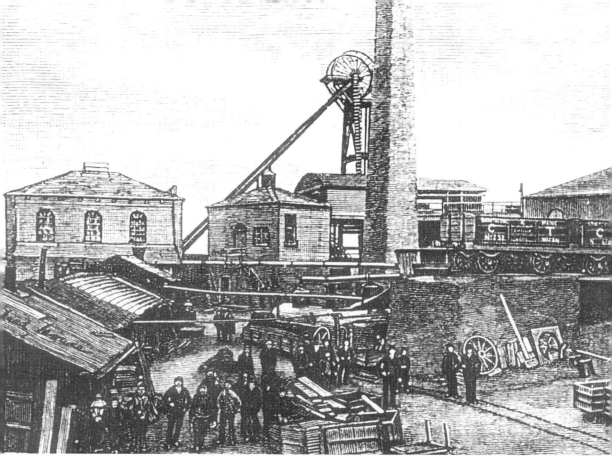

Bamfurlong Colliery on the day of the disaster, 1892. From the Illustrated London News.
www.cmhrc.co.uk

Cross, Tetley and Co. worked the Colliery. The downcast shaft was sunk to a depth of 200 yards to the Pemberton Four Feet Seam. From the bottom, a level roadway ran a distance of about 500 yards, and from here the workings dipped steeply away in a downward direction, at a gradient of about one in four. At the end of the level roadway a compressed air haulage engine was placed in an engine house cut out of the walls of the mine, and framed in wood to support the roof. The dimensions of the engine house was about 6 yards by 4 yards. The purpose of the engine was to haul the coal tubs up the incline; and once the tubs arrived they would be hauled to the shaft bottom by ponies, and then raised to the surface. The haulage engine was fed with compressed air from the surface by means of pipes taken down the shaft, which then ran along the side of the roadways to the engine. Compressed air engines were a popular alternative to steam at this time; however a common problem with them was that the cylinders tended to freeze up by the action of the compressed air. To aleviate this the management authorised the use of a paraffin lamp to be placed under the cylinders. This was not illegal, after all, the fresh air was being drawn into the workings of the mine just 500 yards away, and there would have been no gas to cause an explosion – but it was not gas that was to cause this catastrophe.

At six o'clock on the morning of Wednesday 14 December 1893, fifty men and boys descended the shaft at the Bamfurlong Colliery to begin their day's work. One of these boys, a lad named Rowley, had the job of attending to the haulage engine, and to check that the flame of the paraffin lamp beneath the cylinders was kept properly in flame. It appears that this lamp was not working as it should, and the engine kept stalling and shuddering to a halt. Rowley, aged just fourteen, is supposed to have poured some paraffin over the cylinders of the engine, and then lit it with a lighted torch; or another possibility was that the lamp itself was knocked over – we will now never know. Whatever happened, the events that followed were catastrophic. The oil spread over the floor of the engine room, setting alight the wooden floor, and then the walls of the engine room. The lad tried to extinguish the flames but to no avail. He ran out and tried shouting down to the men working below as the flame and smoke filled the galleries. The fire got an even greater hold and, fanned by the fresh air and the confines of the tunnels, was soon out of control. It burst forth from the engine house and started to eat away at the timbers supporting the roof of the roadway, bringing down the roof of the mine. Down the incline the colliers and the lads employed as drawers were soon made aware that something was wrong – firstly, by the wisps of smoke drifting down, and then by the thicker suffocating smog. They dropped their tools, some dashing up the incline and through the smoke made it into the fresher air beyond the engine house. These, along with a number of others working nearer the shaft bottom, were saved and raised up the pit.

Others down the incline, in a state of panic and self-preservation, decided to run the other way, towards the upcast shaft. This was a mistake. Whether the ventilation was effected by means of a fan or furnace we do not know, but it was working perfectly well, and doing its work, that of drawing the air through the workings. That air was now however was contaminated by the suffocating smoke from the fire, and there was no permanent winding equipment at the upcast shaft. All those who chose this route perished. In one sad case a man named Ashcroft fought this way for a long time, his son at his side, before he had to abandon the lad, lest they both surrendered to death from the effects of the smoke. Some of those who chose to exit by running up towards the engine house also died. The hauling engine, now without power, was at the time hauling up a laden set of tubs. The tubs ground to a halt and then, no longer controlled by the engine, slowly (at first) began to roll back down the incline, gathered speed and then rushed back out of control. Some of the tubs hit the men and boys, other tubs crashed into the roof timbers bringing down more of the roof. On the surface Mr Hutchinson, the manager, was informed of what was happening, and began to make arrangements for a rescue, should any men be left. Colliery managers from the other local pits were also soon at hand to give advice or help with the fire. These included Mr Johnson of the Abram Collieries; Mr Turner from Wigan Junction Collieries; Mr Knowles of Pearson and Knowles, Mr Smith of Ackers, Whitley and Co.; and Mr Robinson of Evans and Co. Following a meeting an ingenious method of extinguishing the fire was formulated. Water was to be sent through the pipes which normally supplied the compressed air to the engine, thus hitting the fire at its source. Men were then sent below with hoses and pumps to tackle the blaze, taking the water from the sump-hole at the bottom of the shaft. Within a few hours the fire was all but out and work could now progress cautiously into the workings. One or two men were found still alive, but these hopeful discoveries were soon changed to disappointment. One after another the bodies of the dead were raised to the surface, the explorations still hampered by smoke and roof falls. The manager, Mr Hutchinson deserves praise in his heroic efforts that day. He was below ground practically all of the time; and even after a period of exhaustion continued to direct operations, advancing into the workings in the thickest of smoke. In the late afternoon he fell and when he was picked up and taken to the surface there were no signs of life. However, in the fresher air he made a faint movement and after some restoratives had been applied recovered enough to be removed to his home. As was normal, large crowds gathered at the pit bank to wait for news. There was, however, none of the normal wailing and crying from relatives, just silent crowds, all waiting. When a roll-call was arranged it was found that sixteen men and boys were missing and dead, named as:

John Cobbett, aged 19, Low Green Road, Platt Bridge
John Dolan, aged 30, Anderton Street, Scholes
Henry Edwards, Spring View, Lower Ince, married
William Bates, aged 14, Heywood Street, Lower Ince
John Ovington, aged 19, Warrington Road, Lower Ince
Joseph Mills, aged 26, Spring View, Lower Ince, married, two children
William Evans, aged 21, Cross Street, Spring View
George Clarey, aged 16, Bamfurlong
John Harrison, aged 31, married, Brackley Street, Walkden
Joshua Mann, Victoria Road, Platt Bridge, married
Charles Mann, son of the above
Michael Cave, aged 16, Lily Lane, Bamfurlong
Simeon Ashcroft, aged 14, Platt Street, Platt Bridge
Richard Fairclough, aged 14, Platt Bridge
William Owen, aged 13, Platt Bridge
James Towey was brought out alive, but died later

At the inquest that followed there was a lengthy summing up and after an hour the jury returned with the following verdict:

We consider all the deceased came to their deaths accidentally. We find the boy, Rowley was not competent to take charge of an engine with an open paraffin torch lamp. We consider it not safe to use an open paraffin torch lamp where the engine is bedded on wood, and where there is a wooden floor. We also recommend that the staple pit be done away with, and that a ladder be placed in it.

The fire occurred at the Bamfurlong No. 1 Pit and four years later this pit was still employing 120 men underground. The other pits at the Bamfurlong Colliery, No. 3 and No. 4, employed 996 men and boys in total at that time. In December 1911, a few days before Christmas, following heavy rain, water from a nearby 'flash' burst through an old shaft and flooded the Bamfurlong Colliery. There were some 'thrilling' escapes according to reports but only one, an old man, was killed through being knocked over and washed away. The foreman, James Green, managed with help from others to save the rest of the men, and was later awarded the Edward Medal. The Bamfurlong Pits were closed down in 1936.

(34) Westleigh Colliery, Westleigh: 20 February 1896

To his horror the cage was raised up with great speed and crashed into the headgearing . . .

We have already noted that the very act of going underground can be fraught with danger, from entering the cage to finishing the shift. Cage or shaft accidents were common in the early years of coal mining. In later years they became a lesser phenomenon, but still happened none the less. In the 1840s it was not uncommon for men and boys, and sometimes girls, to be lowered down the pit shaft in nothing more than a large bucket, often with tragic consequences. We know that in January 1840 Isabella Holme, aged thirteen, Betty Turner, aged eighteen, Thomas Judge, aged ten, James Morris, aged eleven, and Edward Siddon, aged ten were killed by falling from the bucket while descending the pit at Cinders Field Colliery at Wardle near Rochdale. When iron tubs were introduced at the South Hetton Colliery, Co. Durham, this led to the common adoption of cages for carrying the tubs and, of course, the men and boys. There was still a great and constant danger when going down the pit or being raised up. The greatest of these was an 'overwind' whereby the ascending cage was taken up into the headgear over the shaft, sometimes even over the winding wheels into the engine house. In such cases the descending cage plunged either into the water sump at the bottom of the pit or crashed heavily, with fatal consequences, into the thick balks of timber over the sump. A number of inventions prevented overwinds, notably the 'Bryham's Detaching Hooks' and the 'Ormerod Detaching Hooks'. The latter became the more common, in fact almost universal in use in coal mining, and saved many lives. It was invented by Edward Ormerod, an engineer at the Gibfield Colliery, Atherton and patented in 1868. It was first tested the year before, at the Old Chain Pit of the Atherton Collieries. When everything was ready, Mr Ormerod went into the cage himself and shouted to let the cage go down 20 feet. The word was then passed to the engineer to raise the cage up the shaft at full steam. The *Butterfly*, as the detaching hook soon became known, worked and the cage was left hanging over the shaft. The principal of the detaching hook was simple enough. It was attached below the shackle, which attached the winding rope to the cage. Should the cage be overwound, it went up into an iron 'bell', which squeezed the detaching hook, which then uncoupled the rope from the cage. The cage then locked itself above the iron 'bell' and was suspended safely over the shaft.

It appears that there was a detaching hook, but whose invention it was, it is not known, fitted to the cages at the Westleigh Colliery. For whatever reason, this device did not work on this occasion, and the men on board the cage were plunged to their deaths in the shaft.

The Westleigh collieries consisted of a number of pits south of Diggle Flash, the artificial lake created by mining subsidence off the Bickershaw Lane, between Platt Bridge and Tamer Lane End, to the west of Leigh. A short distance to the south-east, was another of the Westleigh Colliery Company's Pits, the Low Hall

Colliery. One of the shafts here was known as the Heyfield Pit or locally as Diggle's Old Seven Foot Pit. The shaft was 445 yards deep, but at the time of this accident the pit was not extensively worked, so only about thirty-six men and boys were employed below ground. Heyfield Pit was abandoned altogether in April 1897, the year after this accident.

The day started as normally on Thursday 20 February 1896. John Prescott, of 142 Firs Lane, Leigh, the banksman, in charge of the cages at the pit top arrived for duty at half-past five that morning. It was still dark, but the top of the shaft was lit up by a number of paraffin lamps. The engine winder, Peter Dickens of Old Fold, Plank Lane was already there. He had begun his work sometime during the night. The cages used at the pit were double decked, allowing two tubs of coal to be placed on each or, when winding men, four men to each deck could accommodated, the men crouched down on their haunches.

Around fifteen minutes to six, the colliers and boys began to arrive to start their day's work, and formed an orderly queue at the shaft top waiting their turn to descend into the pit. The first eight were sent down and as the other cage arrived at the top of the pit it was raised slightly above ground, and then lowered gently on to the 'keps', which held the cage steady. The keps were the metal buffers that were pulled in and out by the banksman by a lever, and kept the cage steady while loading or unloading the men or tubs. When the banksman signalled the winder to lower the cage, the winders first act was to raise it slightly, while the banksman pulled the lever, pulling in and removed the 'keps' thus allowing the cage to descend. The second batch of men and boys entered the cage and were lowered down the pit. All appeared to be working well at this stage. The next cage came from the bottom of the pit and emerged slowly to daylight, ready for the next load of men. This time, the cage 'hung' about a foot above ground, and over the 'keps' but this was not unusual since it would simply bounce a little on the rope as the men entered. The men aboard, the banksman signalled the winder to lower the cage into the pit once more. To his horror the cage was raised up with great speed and crashed into the headgearing, the banksman crying out to the engineman 'Stop!' However, it was too late. The winding ropes acted at the detaching hook, and was uncoupled from the cage; but instead of holding the cage in a safe position it was dropped like a stone, the full depth of the pit, almost 450 yards into the earth.

John Seddon, a collier was working at an inset in the shaft that went to another seam, 315 yards below the surface said that he heard the cage fall, and it went right past the inset where he was working. It crashed through the balks of timber covering the sump, and then out of sight into the water below. One can not even imagine what was going through the minds of the men aboard the cage as they plunged to their deaths. Seddon stated that he heard '*loud cries of agony from the men while the cage was falling*'. There was of course no doubt all aboard the cage had perished, the only available option now was to try and recover the bodies of the unfortunate men from their watery grave far below.

Those who were killed were listed as being:

Henry Dootson, aged 42, bricklayer, Hindley Green, married with one child
Edward Clough, Plank Lane, Leigh, collier, married with five children

Peter Croft, aged 16, taker-off, Scott Street, Wigan Road, Leigh
Edward Farrington, aged 30, Westleigh Lane, married with four children
Joseph Parkinson, aged 25, collier, Hindley Green, single
Walter Cunliffe, aged 26, drawer, 312 Atherton Road, Hindley Green
John Seddon, aged 40, collier, Hindley Green, married with a family
James Hope, aged 22, Ullswater Street, Railway Road, Leigh

Daylight had not yet broken, but news of the disaster soon spread and anxious relatives gathered at the pit bank. The pit manager, Joseph Waterworth and his undermanager, Thomas Arnold descended the pit by another shaft to effect the recovery of the bodies assisted by a number of the colliers. As might be expected all were dreadfully mutilated, stretchers were taken below, and the bodies taken up the pit and removed to the harness room of the nearby Higher Hall Farm which was prepared for use as a temporary mortuary; and there later to be identified by relatives of the poor ill-fated men. Peter Dickens, the engine-winder, was so overcome with the horror at what had happened, that he lay crouched besides the engine room, shaking, mourning and crying in an uncontrollable manner. His mental distress was so great that he was placed under medical care. More scenes of anguish followed at the public inquiry, when Henry Dootson of Smith Lane Hindley Green was called to give evidence. He said:

I am the son of Henry Dootson, one of the men killed, and I was standing on the pit bank when the accident occurred. I left home about twenty minutes to six in the morning. When the cage moved, the man in charge gave a shout, but I heard no more.

There followed an intense inquiry as to why the detaching apparatus did not work and hold the cage in a safe position. The detached rope of the cage was found to be just behind the winding wheel indicating that the winder had stopped the engine as soon as the cage became detached from the rope. Experiments were carried out later at the shaft, and each time the detaching mechanism worked, and the cage held in a safe position. Peter Dickens the engine man was at the inquiry throughout, and at the end was asked by the Coroner if he wished to make a statement, pointing out that it was not necessary for him to do so. Dickens, who looked very ill, said that he preferred to make no statement to the jury. Finally, after a few minutes deliberation, the jury returned the verdict of '*accidental death*'. The reason why the detaching mechanism never worked was never determined, had it worked of course, then all those aboard the cage would have survived. Yet no evidence was taken as to why the cage was drawn up into the detaching apparatus in the first place. This must have been the fault of the engineman, Peter Dickens, as he had full charge of the winding engine that day. The steam was admitted to the engine by a wheel, and the forward and reverse gear was simply a handle, which made the engine work forward and backwards. The engine-winder must of course have to remember which cage was at the top and which was at the bottom. Was it possible that through absent mindlessness Dickens thought that he was lowering the cage, which was already at the bottom, and in doing so raised the other cage into the headgear? This is something we will now never know, but we can be sure it was something that must of played in the mind of Peter Dickens for the rest of his days on earth.

As already noted, the Heyfield Pit where this accident occurred was closed down and abandoned the following year, but the other Westleigh Colliery Cos., Lower Hall No. 2 and Westleigh Pits survived until 1919. At the time of writing the whole area around the former pits is being used as a waste disposal point and very soon it will all be landscaped, leaving no trace whatsoever of the Heyfield Pit, where the eight miners lost their lives. The area around Diggle Flash is even now a pleasant place to be, and a haven for local fishermen and walkers alike, instead of the scenes of industry and death now long gone – how times change!

(35) Hulton Colliery, No. 3 Bank Pit (Pretoria) Westhoughton: 21 December 1910

Such was the force of the blast that the men near the seat of the explosion were found 60 and 70 yards away ...

The area around Hulton Park, Westhoughton, near Bolton was the seat of the Hulton family who from the earliest times had many mining interests in these parts. The Hultons were an influential family. In 1789 William Hulton was the High Sheriff of Lancashire. But it was his son, also named William, who will be remembered as a 'hammer' of the working class, many of whom he employed in his coalmines. This William Hulton, (1787–1864) was born at the family seat, Hulton Park, and educated at Cambridge. He married his cousin, Maria Randle Ford in October 1808 and they had thirteen children, ten of them surviving into adulthood. William's father died in 1800 when William was aged twelve years and when he became of age he inherited the family estate, which included substantial coal mining interests at Hulton Park and Westhoughton. At the age of twenty-four he followed his father to become High Sheriff of Lancashire and, a year later, was called into action at Westhoughton to a cotton mill that was being torched by the Luddites when twelve persons were arrested. Four of these, Abraham Charlston, Job Fletcher, Thomas Kerfoot and James Smith were ordered to be executed. The Charlston family claimed that their lad was only aged twelve years old but he got no reprieve, even though he cried out pitifully for his mother on the scaffold.

By 1819 Hulton had gained a reputation as a man who could and would deal severely with the working class, who at this time were arguing for political reform. In July 1819 he was appointed chairman of the Lancashire and Cheshire Magistrates, a body set up to deal with the social unrest taking place throughout the new industrial northern towns. On 16 July 1819 Hulton and nine others met at a house in Mount Street, Manchester to discuss a planned meeting at St Peter's Field that day. Hulton had already arranged for the military to be present to deal with the large crowd expected to hear Henry Hunt speak on parliamentary reform. The house in Mount Street overlooked St Peter's Field and, after watching events for a number of hours, Hulton decided that 'the town was in great danger'. Hulton then read the Riot Act, and instructed Joseph Nadin, Deputy Constable of Manchester, to arrest Henry Hunt and the other leaders of the demonstration. Nadin said that this could not be done without the help of the military whereupon Hulton then sent two letters to the commander of the military forces in Manchester, and to Major Trafford, the commander of the Manchester and Salford Yeomanry.

It was while the military was following these orders, and making arrests that eleven people were killed and over 4,000 were injured to one degree or another in what became known forever more as the Peterloo Massacre. Hulton never lived down the event in the eyes of ordinary people. Frightened of the abuse that he might receive while campaigning, he turned down a safe Tory seat in the Commons in 1820. The working-class though have long memories, and twenty-two years later, in 1841, he was attacked while campaigning for the Tory candidate for Bolton and had to be rescued by party workers. If he was in any doubt about the reason for the assault, his attackers chanted 'Peterloo – Peterloo', reminding him of the atrocities of 1819. In March 1831 the miners' employed by William Hulton at Westhoughton went on strike. Hulton was furious, he cursed and damned the men and boys, stating that they had betrayed him. He said 'I have amply rewarded you for your labour, relieving you families in sickness and distress, and educated your children. What has been you conduct towards me? You have wantonly injured me in my purse, and have wounded my feelings'. His further comments included '... unions disunite masters and men, and that never again would I employ a member of the Colliers' Union'. This was a base threat which even with all his wealth and power was unable to carry out. As a mine owner Hulton played a large part in the development of the Bolton-Leigh Railway between 1824 and 1828, the object being to get his coal to a wider market and create a shorter, cheaper route to Liverpool. In 1830 this line was linked to the Manchester and Liverpool Railway by Kenyon Junction. William Hulton died in 1864 and was succeeded by his son William Ford Hulton (1811–1879). The Hulton Colliery and the Hulton Park Colliery are listed under the ownership of William Ford Hulton in a mines list for the year 1869.

A glance at the 1844–48 OS map shows that the area around Hulton Park did indeed have a number of coalmines. Hulton Colliery, also known as the 'Chequerbent Pits', was located to the west of Back Gates Farm, and the words 'colliery' and 'coal pits', with a coke works, are shown to the NE of here. There was also a pit near School Farm (School Pit) at this time, and numerous other small mines in the area. However, it is the later pits of the Hulton Colliery Company we are concerned with, in particular the Bank Nos. 3 and 4, being known locally as the 'Pretoria Pits'. These two shafts were sunk between

Advertisement for the Hulton Colliery Company. From Barrett's Directory. Author's collection

1901 and 1902 close to the Westhoughton and Atherton border, but actually in Hulton Park itself, the home of the Hulton family for generations. By 1908 the Hulton Colliery Company was operating pits named 'Deep Half Yard' at Over Hulton, the Bank Nos. 1, 2, 3, and 4 Pits and the Chequerbent No. 1 and 2 Pits, all of which were under the direct charge of manager Alfred James Tonge. The combined employment was 2,277 men and boys, working both underground and on the surface.

The Pretoria Pits, or the Bank Nos. 3 and 4, were each 15 feet in diameter and sunk down to the Arley Mine at a depth of 343 yards from the surface. The shafts were also 70 yards apart. The No. 3 shaft was the upcast where the stale air from the mine was drawn to the surface, and the No. 4 the downcast shaft. From the bottom of the shafts three seams were being worked: the Yard Mine, the Plodder and the Three Quarter Mine. The pits had all the modern equipment necessary to work a mine which was only around ten years old. They had the latest electrical equipment, which included an adequate ventilation system whereby large fans were installed in all the seams. The manager arranged for firemen to make inspections of the workings and to check all the electrical equipment. The results of were recorded in a logbook kept for that purpose.

Early in the morning of 21 December 1910, just three days before Christmas Eve the miners employed at the Pretoria Pit began to make their way to the colliery as they had done on many other days. One old miner even gave his wife a few extra shillings to buy a chicken for the forthcoming festivities before he left for the pit. By seven o'clock all the men and boys were underground. At the No. 3 Pit there were 233 employed in the Yard Mine, ninety in the Plodder Mine and twenty-four in the Three Quarter Mine. At 7.50 am the No. 3 pit was fired by a massive explosion which was heard for miles around. At Westhoughton clocks and other objects were thrown from mantelpieces and foundations shuddered. The mining communities knew full well that the pit had exploded, and soon large crowds gathered at the pithead.

Such was the force of the blast that the men near the seat of the explosion were found 60 and 70 yards away from their place of work, blown there by the detonation of methane gas and coal dust. One man was later found impaled the whole length of his body on a piece of timber; another simply blown in two. The explosion also damaged the shaft lining and jammed the cage in the shaft. As the crowds gathered in the confusion at the pithead during the first half hour there was speculation as to which of the shafts had fired. Some even thought that both pits had exploded, in which case the lives of a further 545 men and boys were in doubt. No attempts could be made to enter the pit until the arrival of the general manager Alfred Joseph Tonge. It was under his directions that the cage and shaft were repaired in just over an hour, at nine o'clock that morning. The manager and five other men chose to enter the workings by means of the No. 4 shaft which itself held several obstacles, but these were slowly cleared away. Some 146 yards down at the entrance to the workings of the Trencherbone Mine, the cage was stopped. There they found the under-manager, Llewellyn Williams. Mr Tonge asked him if he and his men were all right, to which he replied *'Yes, but all are suffering from the fumes of the explosion.'* Williams entered the cage and, after

The colliery manager, Mr Wynne (Mines Inspector) and the under-manager at the Pretoria Colliery on the day of the disaster. Westhoughton Library

The scene at Pretoria Colliery on the day of the disaster, from a postcard. Peter Nadin collection

overcoming more obstacles, they arrived at the Yard Mine, which they then entered. The large electrical ventilation fan here had been blown inwards by the blast, there were roof falls and debris all around. The seam here was also very hot and the afterdamp widespread. Struggling forwards into the workings the rescuers came across a young lad, and then another man, both of whom were sent up the pit. They were the first of many to be found in the No. 4 Pit but those in the No. 3 Pit were not to be so lucky. Returning to the cage, Tonge and his explorers descended down to the Arley Mine where they found scores of men, some with superficial wounds, many weeping from the effects of the afterdamp, thinking that they were about to die, and in anxiety for their loved ones on the surface. The manager ordered that the worst affected men and boys be raised up the shaft first and, after three hours, all 545 men employed at the No. 4 Pit had been raised to the surface using the one cage.

No-one at this time was sure of the fate of any of the men employed in the No. 3 Pit, therefore rescue work began at this shaft. On reaching the Yard Mine the explorers discovered a number of fires and heavy falls of roof. A fireman named Turton was left in charge of putting out the fire, but he was overcome by fumes and died a short time later. The rescue workers had to return to the surface and try to improve the ventilation circuit before further progress could be made, a number of fans being brought into use. Half an hour later the recuers resumed their search but by this time it was obvious that all the men and boys, 344 in number, had perished.

The stench of burnt flesh, smoke and fire filled the air around the pit top at Pretoria Pit; and weeping womenfolk, children, and old men who had gathered there could not take in the consequences of that awful day. They had witnessed the first of many bodies to be brought out of that hell-hole, a youth named Gibson aged just fifteen years. Then a second, thirty-three-year-old Fountain Byers who was still alive but died the following day. To recover all the victims of the Pretoria Pit Disaster from the extremely difficult conditions below ground took until 14 February 1911.

It is little wonder that those of the Westhoughton and district sang no hymns that Christmas – hardy household was spared the terrible grief which only mining communities could witness. One women lost her husband and four sons; a retired collier lost five sons, a nephew and a brother. Others were left to mourn the loss of four or five close relatives. In the houses in Brancker Street, named after two directors of the Hulton Colliery Company, and whose backyards hung over the railway sidings connecting the pit, almost every house had a coffin. The funerals had to follow, and these took place starting on Christmas Day from morning till night and on the days following. There were so many funerals and churches packed to capacity that one young bride had to be married at five o'clock in the morning:

The hearses, the mourning coaches, the long funeral processions, then throngs of bereaved widows and orphans, relatives and friends, the hundreds of visitors, all of them making their way to the last resting places. To see the people in tears, to hear the sobbing and sighing of the wives and children, brothers and sisters, was something beyond human endurance.

The dedication of the memorial near the site of the Pretoria Colliery. Westhoughton Library

These were the words of the rector of the Sacred Heart Church in January 1911. He added:

No-one will ever forget these sights ...

It is indeed gratifying to note that the Westhoughton district has not forgotten those who perished at the Pretoria Pit in December 1910. On the 90th anniversary of the disaster in 2000 the town paid tribute to those who died, as it does on each anniversary. This time it was led by the Mayor and Councillor Janet Halliwell who wore the medal awarded to her great grandfather for his part in the rescue attempts, and also carried the memorial card to his brother who lost his life.

But what was the cause of this disaster? The inquiry began at the Carnegie Hall, Westhoughton on the morning of 20 February 1911, a lengthy and detailed affair with almost 14,000 questions being put forward and answered. The final verdict was as follows:

That on December 21st 1910 at the No. 3 shaft, Bank Pit, commonly known as the No. 3 Pretoria Pit, Westhoughton, an accidental ignition of gas and coal dust occurred when a roof collapsed in the North Plodder Seam, probably due to weakness. The gas was probably ignited by a defective or overheated safety lamp and caused an explosion.

That upon such ignition and explosion there followed a large ignition and explosion of coal dust, affecting all three seams of the No. 3 shaft. All 344 men came to their deaths by accident and not otherwise.

After the probable cause had been found, certain recommendations were made to try and prevent a similar accident, including: (1) There should be more men employed at the mine to deal with safety; (2) Two firemen should be employed instead of one for each shift, and the lamps should be inspected by the firemen who have just come to work on the shift, rather than the firemen who have been working the shift; (3) A proper record of all the lamps used in the mine should be made, and the lamps mended or replaced if they are damaged; and (4) There should be a stronger support of the roof.

The only listed survivors of the Pretoria Colliery Disaster were reported to have been J Sharples, J Staveley, and W Davenport. The rest, 344 men and boys, all perished. Thirteen of the 344 bodies recovered from the Pretoria Colliery Disaster were never identified, and were placed in a tomb at Westhoughton Cemetery, where a large memorial records the disaster, as does a memorial at the Carnegie Hall, Westhoughton. The library here also has a permanent display relating to the Pretoria Disaster to remind future generations of the tragedy. Many years later

A grim but respectful reminder of Lancashire's worst coal mining disaster. Author's Collection

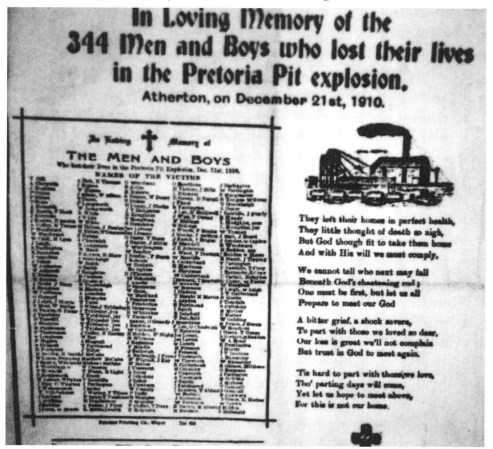

another memorial was placed near the site of the former colliery, so we have not been forgotten those who died in Lancashire's worst mining disaster. This latter memorial lies a few hundred yards away from the capped shafts of the Pretoria Pit which closed in March 1934, but can still be seen – yet another silent witness to events of December 1910.

The Pretoria Colliery Disaster was the greatest single loss of lives in the Lancashire Coalfield and the third greatest mining disaster in British coal mining history. However, it could be argued that the Pretoria Disaster was the *second* greatest disaster in Great Britain. The first was at the Universal Colliery, Wales, in October 1913 which claimed the lives of 439 men and boys. The second greatest is generally accepted as being the Oaks Colliery Disaster at Barnsley, Yorkshire in December 1866, whereby 361 were killed. But this was in *two* explosions and on separate days. When the first explosion occurred it killed 334, ten less than the Pretoria Pit; it was a second explosion the following day that killed twenty-seven rescue men. Whatever the arguments, Pretoria was certainly the greatest *single* English colliery explosion in terms of lives lost.

As always, there are discrepancies in any lists of victims, and this includes those who perished at the Pretoria Pit that day. Those below were listed in the *Reports of the Inspectors of Mines for 1910* under Mr Gerrard's authority:

YARD MINE, AROUND THE SHAFT
Edward Rushton, 36, *under-manager*
John Livesey, 15
Peter Moss, 15
Cyril Cattel, 15
William Green, 14
Dennis Dorcey, 14
Edward Clynes (or Clyns*), 15
John Waring, 14
Alfred E Woods, 14, *lashers on*
William Partington, 40
James Berry, 21, *engineer's Fitter*
Fountain Byers, 33, *pusher-on*
Richard Tonge, 14
Frederick Stanley Houghton, 13
Lewis Hodgkiss (junior), 15, *haulage hands*
Simeon Gibson, 17
Edward Harris, 15
John Oakes (or Jonathan James Oaks*), 13
William Wignall, 14
Mark Critchley, 22
Thomas Faulkner, 15, *hookers on*
James (or John*) Higham, 59, *haulage engineman*

THREE QUARTERS MINE
Frederick Leigh, 36
John Thomas Houghton, 46

Thomas Partington, 24
William Southern, 29
John Roberts, 26
Stephen Hulme, 24
Robert Whittaker, 34 (not listed in relief fund)
Fred Hayes, 43
William Naylor, 16, *lasher-on*
Samuel Hardman, 19
Elias Houghton, 23
James Partington, 42
Thomas Partington (junior), 19
Molyneaux Thomas W, 26
Joseph Topping, 23
William Bond, 28
Richard Sharples, 33
John Austin, 36 (not listed in relief fund)
  all colliers
Thomas Houghton, 17
Anthony Doxey, 18, *drawers*
Thomas Greenhalgh, 60, *back fireman*

NORTH PLODDER (Including Rowland's Tunnel, and Yard Mine)
James Barker, 25 (not listed in relief fund)
Jesse (James*) Chadwick, 23
William Gore, 42

A fund raised a memorial to those who perished in the Pretoria Disaster. Pretoria Collection, Westhoughton Library

Thomas William Brown, 39
William Middlehurst, 47
Joseph Leyland, 24
John Leigh, 42
Henry Blundell, 38
Thomas Smith, 53
James Eccleston, 60
Sydney Dellafield (Delafield*), 25
Peter Higson, 45
William Dawson, 41, *datallers*
James Leigh, 14
John Saunders, 14
Wright Lovett, 15, *lashers-on*
Thomas Hope, 15
William Lees Ashcroft, 15
Edward Houseman, 15 (not listed in relief fund)
Harold Pendlebury, 16
Robert Cowburn, 16, *haulage hands*
John Edward Ernest Hewitt, 45, *electrician*
Gerald Hastie, 19
Thomas Henry Coop, 28
Joseph Horrocks, 19
William Hesketh, 27, *at conveyor*
William Thomas 29, *fireman*
Harry Wyper, 21
Fred Wolstencroft, 39
Samuel Doxey, 25
Thomas Dellafield (Delafield*), 23
Thomas Howcroft, 33
Albert Griffiths, 28
William Cowburn, 42
John Higson, 44
James Seddon, 23
Richard Fairhurst, 47
Albert Holt, 28, *all colliers*
Thomas Martin, 23
Frederick Hook, 14
Albert Unsworth, 17
Fred Pemberton, 18
George Tunstall (junior), 16
John Morris, 21
Edward Saunders, 19
Walter Foster, 28 (not listed in relief fund)
Joseph Atherton, 14
Rowland (Roland*) Evans, 33, *tunneller*
Albert Hardman, 17
Thomas Hastie, 21

William E G Markland, 17, *conveyor attendants*
George Boardman, 23
William Doxey 51, *timberman*
Isaac Ratcliffe, 23, *night fireman*

SOUTH PLODDER DISTRICT
William Turton, 60, *fireman*
Thomas Worthington, 36
Monty Hilton, 29
Orlando Gerrard, 21, *fitter*
Joseph Morris, 13
Albert Roberts, 15
James Livesey, 17 (not listed in relief fund)
William Unsworth, 23
William Hilton, 26, *drawers*
William Bradley, 50
Thomas Jolly (Jolley*), 49
Peter Longworth, 23
John Unsworth, 43
James Hurst, 50 (not listed in relief fund)
William Ratcliffe, 31
James Worthington, 59
Joseph Hilton, 54, *colliers*
Job Ball, 52
James Baxter, 32
Fred Hindle, 22, *datallers*
Walter Woodward, 41, *carpenter*
Percy Hilton, 25
Samuel Partington, 17, *lashers-on*
John Bradley, 21
Joseph Jones, 25
Stanley (Samuel*) Hodgkiss, 14, *haulage hand*
Thomas Hurst, 55
James Unsworth, 30
James Schofield, 37
Richard Green, 53
Richard Light, 45 (38*)
Thomas Ratcliffe, 40
Edward Thomas, 27
Peter Duffy (Duffey*), 24, *pit worker*

YARD MINE (DOWNBROW DISTRICT)
Joseph Darlington, 28
Thomas Loughna (Laughna*), 23
James Hilton, 25
John Baxter (junior), 30

Adam Bullough, 28
Samuel Farrimond, 38
William Potter, 39
Daniel Thomas, 34
John Bullough, 55
John Thomas Aspden, 37
William Kay, 30
Thomas A. Calverbank (Calderbank*), 23
Walter Mead, 49
William Schofield, 32
Edward Hollingworth (Hollingsworth*), 33
William Golding, 36
Martin Marrin, 31
Albert Norman, 37
Thomas Dunn, 34
Joseph Miller, 31
William Hollingworth, 33
William Ashton, 22
Paul Thomasson (Thomason*), 45
Richard Golding, 34
Thomas Greenhalgh, 24
John Rushton, 32 (not listed in relief fund)
Walter (William*) Vickers, 28
John Coffey, 28
Albert Smith, 25
William Hayes, 28
Richard Longmate, 29
Thomas Hurst, 48
William Brumley (Bromby*), 37
John Tyldesley senior, 53
James Paulding, 21 (31*)
David Nuttall, 23
Percival Monks, 36
Joseph Greenall, 34
John Topping, 54
Harry Miller, 32
Richard Mather, 49
Israel Bennett, 24
William Eccleston, 20
Arthur Chetwynd (Chetwyn*), 21
Isaac Smith, 30 (not listed in relief fund)
Walter Aspden, 28
Edward Haynes (Haines*), 35
Thomas Woodward, 33
Thomas Gill, 22
Joseph Higham, 23

Thomas Yates, 30
Daniel Simmonds (Simmons*), 21
Herbert Vickers, 22
Walter Leigh, 21
John Prestcott, 23 (not listed in relief fund)
Fred Balforn, 30
Herbert Prescott, 24 (not listed in relief fund)
James Mills, 26
Ralph Crostan (Croston*), 25
Leonard (Emmanuel*) Emmett, 18
Joseph Tyldesley, 17 (not listed in relief fund)
Thomas Aldred (Aildred*), 14
John Robert Hargreaves, 27
James (Joseph*) Farrimond, 15
Albert Howarth, 16
William Anderton, 15
James Holden (Holdick*), 15, *haulage hands*

One of a number of memorials to the Pretoria disaster, this example located near the site of the colliery. Author's collection

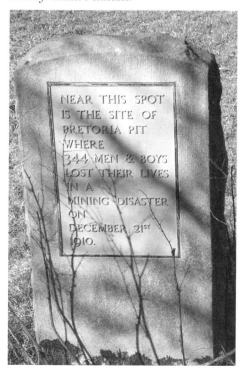

The capped shafts at the former Pretoria Colliery. Author's collection

Joseph Scoble, 53 (not listed in relief fund)
Edward Tumblety (John Tumbley*), 20
Percy Woodward, 18, *all datallers*
James Lovett, 28
Mark Skeldon, 28
Charles Wharton, 36
John Baxter (senior), 58
David Grundy, 48
John Boardman, 31
William Shambley, 28
James Hodgkiss, 31
James (Joseph*) Price, 42
Nicholas Hartley, 44
John Parr, 51
Samuel Woodward, 34
Daniel Mather, 23
James Eccleston, 31
Ambrose Coffey, 24
Fred Dootson, 26
James Morris, 29
John Houghton, 45
Frederick Coffey, 30

Peter Green, 41
Fred Southworth, 22
Richard Thomasson (Thomason*), 51
William Rigby, 53
William Smith, 46
Peter Leigh, 49
George Sharples, 58 (not listed in relief fund and may be 'J Sharples', a survivor of the blast)
Edward Mather, 35
Thomas Howcroft, 25
Thomas Bennett, 22 (17*)
Samuel Critchley, 29
Benjamin While (White*), 20
James Seddon, 21
William Tyldesley, 28
Abel Mangnall (Magnall*), 24
George Tanstall senior
Ralph Shaw, 35
Samuel Baxter, 24
Thomas Greenall, 36
William Jolley, 26
Walter Mangnall (Magnall*), 31

John Tyldesley, 25
Fred Schofield, 2, *all colliers*
Thomas Tyldesley, 23 (17*)
Arthur Aspden, 21
George Potter, 16
Enoch Arthur Bates, 23
Henry Bennett, 20 (not listed in relief
    fund)
William Bellew (Bellow*), 19
George Henry Parks, 19
Richard Lawrence Spencer, 28
George Williams, 25
Henry (Joseph*) Dootson, 24
John Flood, 27
Edward Halliwell Green, 22
Thomas Hurst, junior, 19
John Monks, 19
Oliver (Walter*) Southern, 21
William Calderbank, 21
Joseph McCabe, 22
Samuel Wharmby, 26
Thomas Charles Faulkner, 25, *all drawers*
Alfred Edward (Arthur*) Woods, 15
James Potter, 15

Walter Crook, 16
Moses Turner, 21
James Ernest Withington, 13
John Smith, 43
Joseph Lovett, 50
Robert Calderbank, 23
John Hundy, 52, *fireman*

YARD MINE (EAST JIG DISTRICT)
Orlando Chadwick (Calderbank*), 42
William Morris, 34
Edward Kenwright, 28
Thomas Horrocks, 49
Enoch Pemberton, 29
John Thomas Dootson, 26
Wilfred Seddon, 20
John L. Pemberton, 21
Harry Doxey, 23, *drawers*
James Feeley (Fetley*), 40
Joseph Grundy Battersby, 16, *haulage
    hand*
Alfred Calderbank, 49, *fireman*
Walter Boardman, 28
Frederick Teasdale (Teesdale*), 40

Pretoria Colliery, from a postcard. Peter Nadin collection

Believed to be the upcast shaft at Pretoria Colliery soon after the disaster. From a postcard. Peter Nadin collection

William Croston, 38
John Andrew Wise, 44
Robert Morris, 43
John Morris, 36, *all colliers*
Herbert Gibson, 19
Richard Seddon, 24
Michael Malloy (Molloy*), 26
Thomas Emmett, 32, *datallers*
Robert Clifford Curwen, 19 (not listed in relief fund)

TOP YARD DISTRICT
James Miller, 50
Matthew Seddon (senior), 45
Henry Price, 22 (not listed in relief fund)
Samuel Thornley, 25
James McDonald, 27
Henry Holden (Holding*), 31
William Evans, 26
Willie Riding (Rydings*), 22
Samuel Dootson, 30

George Sargeant, 28
Ben Davies, 23
John (Joe*) Hodson, 40
James Tyrer, 49
Thomas Farrimond, 41, *all colliers*
Fred Ratcliffe (Alfred Radcliffe*), 21
Joshua Leigh (Lee*), 22
Matthew McCabe, 24
Benjamin Riding (Rydings*), 19
Thomas Gibbs, 26
Robert Cope, 19
Lewis Hodgkiss (senior), 39, *fireman*
Samuel Cowburn, 52
Robert Roberts, 22
James (Joseph*) Clarke, 23
Richard Jolly (Jolley*), 24
Joseph Partington, 25
Matthew Seddon (junior), 24
Thomas Green, 28
Thomas Owen (Came*), 26
Albert Lonsdale, 37

James Green, 35
William Dykes, 39
Thomas Marsh, 50
William Catterall, 40
Harry Partington, 19
Michael McCabe, 20
Albert Shambley, 17
Andrew Lowe, 23

Robert Marsh, 20
Joseph Seddon, 18, *all drawers*
James Edward Hogan, 15, *haulage hands*
Samuel Hundy, 39, *fireman*

ARLEY MINE
Richard Clayton, 55, *fireman*

The grave of Richard Nelson (Longmate), son of George Henry and Jane Longmate 'who lost his life at the Pretoria Colliery explosion, December 21st 1910, aged 29 years'. His grave can be seen in the churchyard of St Stephen, Kearsley Moor. Author's collection

The above list actually names 337 men and boys but it is known that 344 perished. There were, however, three survivors of the blast, which would make this list complete. But there are also a number of other anomalies and, entries marked thus*, are taken from a separate list in the Relief Fund document held at Westhoughton Library, giving the names etc., as marked there. While researching the disaster at the Unity Brook Colliery I also came across, quite by accident, the grave of Richard Nelson (Longmate), son of George Henry and Jane Longmate who *Lost his life at the Pretoria Colliery Explosion, December 21st 1910, aged 29 years*. His grave can be seen at the Church of St Stephen, Kearsely Moor. Richard's parents show up in the 1881 census returns at 271 Manchester Road, Kearsley, where his father's occupation is listed as being a carpenter. The year 1881 would have been when Richard would have been born when little did his parents know of the terrible fate that lay before him twenty-nine years later.

In August 2004 Bolton Museum was able to purchase the Edward Medal awarded to the colliery manager, Alfred Tonge, for his efforts in the rescue attempts on the day of the Pretoria Colliery Disaster. Ten other Edward Medals were awarded for acts of bravery at the colliery that day.

Select bibliography

Francis, James J, *Bradshaw and Harwood Collieries*, Turton Local History Society, 1982.

Mining Disasters of the Leigh Area, edited by Tim Macquiban and Norman Acker, Leigh Local History Society, Publication No. 3, 1975.

Morley, M A, *A Study of the Pretoria Pit Disaster on 21 December 1910 at Westhoughton, Lancashire* (thesis, 1978), Bolton Local Studies Library.

Nadin, J, *Happy Valley No More*, 2001 (Hapton Valley Colliery).

Tootle, H, *The Moorfield Pit Disaster*, 1998, Landy Publishing.

Simm, G and Winstanley, I, *Mining Memories: An Illustrated Record of Coal Mining in St. Helens*, 1990, St Helens MBC.

Winstanley, I, *The Unfortunate Colliery: High Brooks, Park Lane, Ashton-in-Makerfield, Lancashire*, Picks Publications.

Winstanley, I, *With Hearts so Light. The story of the Queen Pit Explosion, Haydock 1868 and July 1869.* Picks Publications.

Wood, K, *The Coal Pits of Chowbent*, 1984, UPS Blackburn Ltd.

Glossary

Afterdamp A mixture of non-inflammable gasses left after a 'methane explosion' in a coal mine. Afterdamp was responsible for more deaths among miners than actual physical injuries due to explosions.

Banksman The person in charge of the shaft and cage or 'skip' at the surface of the colliery.

Cage The 'lift' at the shaft whereby men and materials were lowered into the workings; also used for the raising of coal from the pit.

Chock A roof support of rectangular blocks of wood placed alternately from the floor of the coal seam to the roof of the mine. In later years the term used for hydraulic roof supports.

Chokedamp A mine gas consisting of carbon dioxide.

Collier A person who actually gets and hews the coal at the coalface. It its earliest form 'coalier'.

Dataller A general underground labourer on a fixed daily wage.

Downcast The shaft at a colliery where the fresh air was drawn into the workings to replace the foul air and gasses. This was achieved in the early days by a furnace or fire at another shaft, and in later years by fans.

Drawer A person (usually a youth) who draws (eg pushes) coals in tubs from the coalface to the shaft or to a haulage point to be removed from the surface. Also known as a 'trammer' in Yorkshire.

Face More properly 'coalface', the place where the coal is actually got from a coal seam or seams.

Fan See 'Ventilation fan'.

Filler A person who fills the tubs of coal or loads it onto a conveyor after the coal has been blasted, cut or brought down by hand-pick.

Firedamp The explosive gas (in certain quantities) released from coal seams, the cause of many colliery explosions.

Fitter A mechanic or person with mechanical knowledge employed underground at a colliery, responsible for the repair, maintenance and installation of machinery.

Furnace See 'Ventilation furnace'.

Gob *or* **Goaf**	The waste, or space left after the coal has been extracted, which was usually allowed to 'drop'. Likened to pulling the filling (the coal) out of a sandwich and allowing the bread (the roof) to fall together.
Headgear	Often regarded as the symbol of the mining industry; the wood or steel frame above a mine shaft with wheels fixed on top for raising and lowering men and materials, and the coal itself.
Hooker-on	A haulage-hand employed underground who 'hooked-on' (or attached) the coal tubs and materials going into the mine onto a moving haulage rope – occasionally with the loss of a finger or two!
Hopper	A bunker or storage for coal, either underground or on the surface.
Hoppet	A large bucket attached to the winding rope at a shaft usually used during shaft sinking or to provide emergency access to the workings, such as where damage was done to the cages during an explosion or other accident.
Haulage-hand	A person employed underground or on the surface in connection with the conveyance of coal, equipment or materials. Could also be employed turning the coal tubs around at a junction or uncoupling chains from the haulage rope.
Jinney	A haulage engine.
Jigger	An underground haulage engine operator. In Lancashire also known as a 'ginney tenter'.
Keps	Steel blocks on which the cage rests when at the top of the shaft to keep it steady. The cage is raised slightly above the shaft top, the keps are put in place by a man perating a lever, and the cage is then lowered.
Lasher-on	See 'Hooker-on'.
Level	A horizontal tunnel underground in the mine.
Metal-man	The person employed to remove rock and waste from the mine. In Lancashire called a 'tunneler'.
Naked light	A lit candle or candles or other exposed flames used in oil lamps.
Ostler	A person in charge of the pit ponies.
Overlooker	A mine official employed to oversee a district underground; also known as an overman, his status between a fireman and a manager.
Pit bank	The surface area of a colliery around the shaft top and its immediate surroundings.

Pony driver	A person, usually a youth, in charge of a pit pony or ponies employed in the haulage of coal and materials underground.
Prop	A wood or metal roof support.
Safety lamp	A form of naked lighting which is safe to be used underground, being protected from igniting any inflammable gases by gauzes and glass, the Davy flame lamp being a famous example.
Stemming	Clay or similar material which is rammed into a shot-firing hole to stop the shot (the explosive) being fired out of the hole, making optimim use of the explosives used.
Stopping	A permanent or temporary obstruction placed in a mine tunnel to direct the flow of air through the mine. Also the term used for the complete blockage to the old workings of a mine.
Timber-man	A person employed to take wooden supports and other materials to the coalface; also known in Lancashire as 'supply workers' or 'tackle-lads'.
Underlooker	A term (common in the nineteenth century) for the person employed to supervise the underground operations of a coal mine, directly under the manager. Also known as the undermanager.
Upcast	The shaft at the colliery where the stale air was drawn to the surface by a furnace or a fan.
Ventilation fan	The mechanical means of extracting the air from the mine via the upcast shaft, to be replaced by fresh air drawn from the downcast shaft.
Ventilation furnace	An early form of mine ventilation whereby a furnace (a contained, controlled fire) was placed at the bottom of the shaft, the heated air then rising up the shaft, and drawing cleaner and fresher air in to the working by another shaft at the pit. It was not uncommon in the early days of mine for a single shaft to operate but this could be divided into two to obtain a similar though not fully effective result.

Index